Contents

Preface

The *Global Industry Standard for Tailings Management* was launched on 5 August 2020, at the height of the COVID-19 pandemic. The authors of this book were participants in the development of the Standard. This enables us to provide insights into the origins of the Standard that we hope will be of interest to all who have a stake in the performance of the mining industry.

For us, the rapid development of a global standard was an exhilarating, rewarding, frustrating, infuriating, all-absorbing experience, which helps explain some of the tone in which this book is written. It is not an academic treatise, but a passionate account that reflects our commitment to the task. Of course, we intend this passion to be tempered by reason. Whether we succeed is for others to say. The authors are 2 of the so-called "expert panel" of 7 who were recruited to construct a draft of the Standard. The other members of the panel are in no way responsible for this account. It is our personal perspective, highlighting matters in which we are most interested. Other panel members would no doubt have chosen different matters to highlight.

The process by which the Standard was created came to be known as the *Global Tailings Review*, frequently shortened here to GTR. Readers who want a comprehensive discussion of the GTR process are encouraged to consult the account written by those who managed it.[1]

We need to declare our position on the Standard at the outset. It is the product of a political process. That means it is fundamentally a compromise by all involved. It is not something that any one person or interest group would have written left to themselves.

Members of the expert panel were recruited to provide ideas and technical input. Some of those ideas are incorporated into the Standard but some were rejected as part of the process of compromise that led to the final version. Given that we were recruited for our expertise, it is not surprising that we continue to hold many of the ideas we brought to the table. We are therefore critical of certain aspects of the Standard, as well as the process by which it was created.

On the other hand, we believe the Standard, if implemented effectively (and that is a big if – see Chapter 11) could produce a major step change in tailings facility safety. The metaphor of a step change suggests that there are further steps along this path. The Standard is part of a journey that is not yet complete. In short, we are advocates for the Standard, as well as for the improvements that we hope will come in time.

Our book is not an exposition of the Standard. To know what the Standard contains there is no substitute for reading it (Appendix 3) as well as some of the accompanying explanatory writings.[2] This book is an account of the process by which the Standard

---

[1] Oberle, B, Mihaylova, A and Hackett, A, Global Tailings Review at a Glance: History and Overview, *Towards Zero Harm: A Compendium of Papers Prepared for the Global Tailings Review*, Chapter I. www.globaltailingsreview.org/wp-content/uploads/2020/09/Ch-I-Global-Tailings-Review-at-a-Glance_History-and-Overview.pdf.

[2] Oberle, B and Brereton, D, (Eds) *Towards Zero Harm: A Compendium of Papers Prepared for the Global Tailings Review*, www.globaltailingsreview.org/compendium/. Hereafter the *GTR Compendium*.

was constructed and of some of the contentious issues the expert panel had to deal with.

In writing this book, we followed the Chatham House Rule. Adherence to the rule was agreed amongst the chair and the expert panel in the earliest stages of the process. This permits us to discuss the internal workings of the review, while refraining from identifying individuals. Mostly we cite public domain materials. We otherwise cite sources that were circulated widely or provided to us by people outside the review process. We were privy to an enormous amount of highly confidential information during the review, which we have treated as strictly confidential. It is from within these parameters that we have sought to bring readers as close to the GTR process as we were.

We, the authors, are both sociologists. One of the key concepts of our discipline is power. This is therefore a study of power – who had it, how it was exercised and with what effect. As the book title suggests, it is a political analysis of how the Standard came into being.

The word "we" is used repeatedly in this book. To avoid confusion, we restrict its use to we, the authors of this book, and speak of the expert panel, of which we were members, in the third person (the panel, it, etc). Very occasionally, "we" refers to a triad: the authors together with you, the reader.

The various sections of the book were initially drafted by one or other of us, and then edited by both. We are jointly responsible for all opinions expressed.

Finally, we have learned an enormous amount about the mining sector, the investment and insurance industries, multi-lateral and state processes, and the perspectives of people affected by mining, including the experiences of victims who suffered great loss from Brumadinho and other tailings disasters. Many people bravely voiced their views and opinions to the expert panel, even when they disagreed with the process or the content of our drafts. The opportunity to participate in the panel, to listen and weigh options, to debate the best course of action with others, and to influence the outcome, was indeed a privilege.

Andrew Hopkins and Deanna Kemp

January 2021

About the Authors

Deanna Kemp is a Professorial Research Fellow, University of Queensland, Brisbane.

Contact: d.kemp@smi.uq.edu.au

Deanna has worked at the University of Queensland's (UQ) Sustainable Minerals Institute (SMI) since 2005. She is Director of the SMI's Centre for Social Responsibility in Mining (CSRM), a leading centre of applied social research in the extractive industries. Before UQ, she worked for a global mining company.

Through a diverse set of collaborations, Deanna's research focuses on company-community conflict, displacement and resettlement, and human rights and development. She also examines how the global mining industry is organised, resourced and incentivised to respond to these and other social justice challenges. She covers many of these themes in *Extractive Relations: Countervailing Power and the Global Mining Industry*, a book co-authored with Professor John Owen.

Deanna holds a PhD from UQ. She is one of a limited number of social scientists who combines critical scholarship with close industry and community engagement. She pushes the boundaries of these engagements to support change and industry reform.

Andrew Hopkins is Emeritus Professor of Sociology, Australian National University, Canberra.

Contact: andrew.hopkins@anu.edu.au

Andrew was an expert witness at the Royal Commission into the 1998 Exxon gas plant explosion near Melbourne. He was a consultant to the US Chemical Safety Board in its investigation of the BP Texas City Refinery disaster of 2005, and also for its investigation into the BP Gulf of Mexico oil spill of 2010. He has written books about these accidents, with over 100,000 copies sold.

He has been involved in various government reviews of Work Health and Safety regulation and regulators and has done consultancy work for major companies in the mining, petroleum, chemical and electrical industries, as well as for the Defence Force. He speaks regularly to audiences around the world about the human and organisational causes of major accidents.

- BSc and MA from Australian National University, PhD from University of Connecticut.

- Winner of the 2008 European Process Safety Centre safety award, the first in time it was awarded to someone outside Europe.

- Honorary fellow of the Institution of Chemical Engineers in recognition of his "outstanding contributions to process safety and to the analysis of process safety related incidents".

- Life member of the Australian Institute of Health and Safety and has received its highest award for "lifetime achievement".

- Member of the advisory board of NOPSEMA – the Australian National Offshore Petroleum Safety and Environmental Management Authority.

- Officer of the Order of Australia (AO) in recognition of his "distinguished service to industrial safety and accident analysis".

Books by Andrew Hopkins

Making Safety Work (Allen & Unwin, 1995)

Managing Major Hazards: The Moura Mine Disaster, (Allen & Unwin, 1999)

Lessons from Longford: The Esso Gas Plant Explosion (CCH, 2000)

Lessons from Longford: The Trial. (CCH, 2002)

Safety, Culture and Risk (CCH, 2005)

Lessons from Gretley: Mindful Leadership and the Law, (CCH, 2007)

Learning from High Reliability Organisations (CCH, 2009). Edited

Failure to Learn: the BP Texas City Refinery Disaster (CCH, 2008)

Disastrous Decisions: Human and Organisational Causes of the Gulf of Mexico Blowout (CCH, 2012)

Nightmare Pipeline Failures: Fantasy planning, black swans and integrity management (CCH, 2014). With Jan Hayes

Risky Rewards: The Effect of Company Bonuses on Safety (Ashgate, London, 2015) with Sarah Maslen

Quiet Outrage: The Way of a Sociologist (CCH: Sydney, 2016)

Organising for Safety: How Structure Creates Culture. (CCH: Sydney, 2019)

Abbreviations

ALARP	As low as reasonably practicable
CRO	Chief risk officer
DSR	Dam safety reviews
GTR	Global Tailings Review
FPIC	Free, prior and informed consent
ICMM	International Council for Mining and Metals
ICOLD	International Commission on Large Dams
IFC	International Finance Corporation
MAC	Mining Association of Canada
NGO	Non-governmental organisation
OECD	Organisation for Economic Co-operation and Development
PRI	Principles for Responsible Investment
UNEP	United Nations Environment Program

"My parents did not deserve to have to bury their own daughter and to have to live with this pain for the rest of their lives. The lives that were taken and the destruction that took place could have been avoided. It's time for the mining sector to stop being all about profit, and act with humanity."

Angélica Amanda Andrade

Angélica's older sister worked for Vale and was killed in the Brumadinho tragedy with hundreds of others. Angélica is now a community advocate seeking justice for the families affected by the tragedy.

CHAPTER 1

Introduction

On 25 January 2019, a tailings dam in Brazil failed, releasing a mudflow that killed 270 people. The dam was owned by global mining company, Vale. Nearly all of those who died were employees having lunch in a canteen below the dam wall. The dam was situated about 9 kms from Brumadinho, the town that has given its name to the disaster. The dam itself was known simply as Dam 1 at the Feijão mine. It had not received any tailings since 2016, but had remained in a precarious state for the subsequent 3 years, before it collapsed.

Brumadinho is the world's worst tailings dam failure, in terms of lives lost, just eclipsing the failure of a dam at Stava in Italy in 1985, in which 268 people lost their lives.

The failure was also an environmental disaster, although not Brazil's worst. Four years earlier, a tailings dam collapse at the nearby Samarco mine killed 19 people and polluted a river system all the way to the sea, nearly 900 kms away, damaging the livelihood of hundreds of thousands of people. This was Brazil's worst-ever mining-related environmental disaster. Samarco was half-owned by Vale. Subsequent to the Samarco failure, Vale's new CEO declared that the company's motto would be "never again".[1] Yet, it *had* happened again.

The Brumadinho disaster was the last straw for many mining industry stakeholders. It was the most recent in a long line of tailings dam disasters. Like all the others, it was a disaster that should not have happened, attributable to bad management and poor engineering practices. The credibility of the industry was in tatters. Communities directly affected by these tragedies and the non-governmental organisations (NGOs) who represent them were irate, demanding that governments take action. Investors began divesting from Vale. The mining industry metaphorically hung its head in shame.

This was an unprecedented situation for the mining industry, requiring an unprecedented response. That response was a decision to create an independent tailings management Standard, to which the major mining companies would commit and with which other companies would be encouraged to comply. The Standard had 3 co-conveners – first, the peak mining industry association, the International Council for Mining and Metals (ICMM), second, a group of ethical investors, the Principles for Responsible Investment (PRI) and third, the United Nations Environment Program (UNEP). All 3 would have to endorse the Standard. Industry hoped this would give it the credibility necessary to convince investors that their investments were secure, and to convince governments that they did not need to impose tougher rules on the industry. A complex set of organisational arrangements was developed to ensure that the Standard would represent as far as possible the interests of all stakeholders, not just the industry. One aspect of these

---

1 Bautzer, T, New dam disaster puts Vale CEO, deals and dividends under scrutiny, *Reuters*, 28 January 2019. reuters.com/article/us-vale-sa-disaster-strategy-analysis/new-dam-disaster-puts-vale-ceo-deals-and-dividends-under-scrutiny-idUSKCN1PM08A.

arrangements was the recruitment of an independent panel of experts, of which we were members, to help with drafting the Standard. This book is the story of that process.

What is a tailings dam?

Large tailings dams are the largest engineered structures on the planet. And when they fail, they can cause massive death and destruction.

Tailings are a by-product of hard rock (ie metalliferous) mining.[2] The rock from the mine must be crushed and then subject to various mechanical and chemical processes to extract the metals or ores of interest. The waste material is known as tailings and is usually discharged as slurry and piped to a storage location known as a tailings storage facility or dam.[3]

Tailings are a waste product, and companies have historically sought to dispose of them as cheaply as possible, sometimes dumping them in rivers without any consideration of their effects on the environment or on people downstream. There is a close parallel here with the burning of fossil fuels. The by-product, carbon dioxide, has historically been discharged into the atmosphere without concern for the long-term consequences. And now, just as companies are being asked to take responsibility for the greenhouse gases they produce, mining companies are being required to dispose responsibly of their unwanted tailings.

The problem of tailings storage is becoming progressively worse for 2 reasons. First, the world is consuming ever-increasing volumes of the metals being produced. But second, technological advances mean that lower and lower grade ores can be mined economically. In turn, this means an ever-increasing volume of waste for each tonne of metal produced.

Tailings dams differ from water storage dams in various respects. A water storage dam is initially built to its final height, after which it is commissioned and then filled with water over a period that may take years. A tailings dam is built in stages or "raises", which consist of embankments made of earth and stone. Tailings are piped in behind the embankment with much of the water slowly draining away. When each stage is full, the next is constructed, more or less on top of the first, but often resting in part on already deposited tailings.[4] And so on, almost indefinitely. When no longer in use, tailings dams are supposed to be closed or finished off, in such a way that they are safe in perpetuity, unable to rupture or to leak toxic substances.

However, there is a long history of tailings dam failures, both of dams that are still being filled with tailings, and of dams that are no longer in use. Some of these failures have caused many deaths, some have caused none, but nearly all have caused environmental damage. A compilation of "major tailings dam failures" records 66 such failures between 1995 and mid-2020, an average of 2.6 failures per year. There

---

2 This discussion is not directly applicable to coal mining.
3 We use these expressions interchangeably here, although for some purposes they need to be distinguished.
4 We discuss construction methods in more detail in Chapter 6.

was at least one failure every year during this 25-year period with the highest number being 6 in 2019. The compilers of the list caution that it is in no way complete.[5]

Chapter outline

Given that the Brumadinho disaster was the catalyst for the new Standard, Chapter 2 gives a more detailed account of the factors that contributed to this failure. The chapter draws heavily on an independent report of the accident, which covers both technical and organisational causes. The technical causes of tailings dam failures have been much studied; less so, the organisational causes. The report's discussion of organisational causes is therefore particularly valuable. We use this discussion to identify lessons for prevention. Since the Standard is intended to prevent any more "Brumadinhos", this chapter also considers the extent to which the "lessons of Brumadinho" are incorporated in the Standard.

Chapter 3 deals with the industry's unfolding credibility crisis that culminated in the decision to create a global Standard for the management of tailings facilities. The crisis developed slowly, over many years, with steady pressure for the industry to adopt principles for sustainable mining. The crisis intensified after the Samarco disaster of 2015. UNEP issued a report that suggested obliquely that tailings dam technologies were too dangerous and needed to be phased out. It also proposed stronger regulation by the state. Investor groups began lobbying the ICMM to introduce a safety Standard for tailings dams.

But Brumadinho was the tipping point. Six days after the accident, investors made a public call for a new safety Standard, to be developed independently of industry. Some of ICMM's member companies publicly supported this call. A month later, the ICMM committed itself to such a Standard. It recognised that:

> "To be a credible process it needs to be multi-stakeholder. A wholly industry-owned process will not be regarded as credible and will therefore serve no purpose." (See Appendix 1)

Accordingly, it invited UNEP and the investor group, PRI, to co-convene the process. The Standard would need to be carefully negotiated among these 3 organisations, and each would have veto rights. From the ICMM's point of view, the development of the Standard would be a balancing act. The industry would need to relinquish some degree of control over how it operated, while at the same time protecting its fundamental interests. How this was done is the subject of Chapter 4.

Chapter 4 notes that the development of the Standard was ostensibly based on 2 principles. The first was that the 3 co-conveners were formally equals, wielding equal decision-making power. The second was that the initial drafting by the expert panel was to be conducted in an independent manner. Neither of these principles was adhered to. The ICMM, in reality, always believed its views should carry greater weight than the views of the other 2 co-conveners. Moreover, it frequently sought to exert pressure on the expert panel. Indeed, it exercised a unilateral veto of some of the panel's proposals even before the other 2 co-conveners had a chance to consider

---

5 WISE Uranium Project, *Chronology of major tailings dam failures*, 25 September 2020. wise-uranium. org/mdaf.html.

them. The development of the Standard was in fact a political process in which ICMM fought to preserve the material interests of its members as far as possible, while UNEP and PRI struggled to give substance to the principle that safety came first. The ICMM argued again and again that its positions were the only realistic ones and that any attempt to set higher standards would mean that companies would refuse to sign up to the Standard. More often than not, this argument for "realism" won the day.

As agreement among the co-conveners on the Standard came closer, a mining industry disaster of a different kind occurred. Rio Tinto destroyed 2 rock shelters at Juukan Gorge in Western Australia that contained evidence of human habitation dating back 46,000 years. It did so knowingly and against the wishes of the traditional owners. This was, among other things, a public relations disaster for the company receiving worldwide media coverage. It was also a demonstration of the importance of the UN principle that mining activities that affect indigenous people should be dependent on their "free, prior and informed consent" (FPIC).

Interestingly, the destruction of the Juukan Gorge rock shelters had a direct impact on the final content of the Standard. It motivated UNEP to take stronger positions in the final stages of negotiations, on issues such as FPIC. For this reason, we refer to the Juukan Gorge matter at various points in this book.

We are sometimes asked how the expert panel operated. Chapter 5 provides a very brief answer. The panel was a small group and, as such, exhibited many of the features of small group behaviour. We describe some of this behaviour and how it influenced the content of the Standard.

The remaining chapters deal with some of the substantive issues that were debated during the construction of the Standard and identify the political processes that led to the final outcome in each case.

Chapter 6 concerns the question of scope. The Standard consists of a set of requirements that companies are expected to implement. The initial scoping document explicitly prevented the expert panel from proposing requirements that certain types of dam construction be prohibited, or that certain types of disposal methods be prohibited, such as dumping tailings in rivers (see Appendix 1). Nevertheless, we consider these matters here because they reveal some of the ways in which power was exercised during the construction of the Standard.

Beyond these exclusions, there were other matters that the ICMM argued should be out of scope, but on which it could not insist. For example, it wanted to restrict the scope to requirements that would minimise the risk of *sudden* tailings dam failures. The other 2 co-conveners and the expert panel argued that the scope should include, amongst other things, *chronic* failures, such as the leakage of toxic materials into water supply systems and the failure of companies to properly close dams when no longer in use, leading to slow environmental disasters, if not rapid ones. The rights of project-affected people were also outside the scope of the Standard, as initially imagined by the ICCM, but very much within scope as far as others were concerned. These matters were hotly contested, leading sometimes to surprising outcomes.

Chapter 7 deals in detail with the protection of project-affected people, particularly indigenous peoples, from tailings facility failures. It describes the struggle over whether the Standard should contain any requirements at all for protecting the rights of affected communities, a struggle which led eventually to these requirements being positioned prominently at the beginning of the Standard. Two substantive issues proved very controversial. The first was whether affected communities should be able to participate in decisions about the construction and management of tailings dams. As a result of various wording compromises, the meaning of the requirement in question was quite unclear in the final version. The second issue was the extent to which mining companies should be required to *obtain* the free, prior and informed consent of affected indigenous communities. The final wording requires that companies *work to obtain* such consent. This is a major concession to the ICMM since all that companies need do to comply is show that they *tried* to obtain consent. NGOs, indigenous people and their advocates have expressed disappointment with these outcomes.

Chapter 8 deals with issues of accountability and governance. Without clear accountabilities for the safety of tailings facilities, there is a risk that the drive to maximise production will overwhelm good engineering practices. The Standard does not require that company boards be held accountable in this matter; the chapter explains why. On the other hand, the board itself can structure accountability for safety into a mining company. There are several inter-related elements required. First, there should be a dedicated position on the corporate executive accountable for safety. Second, tailings engineers should report up a functional line to this executive. Third, any bonuses paid to these people in this line should reflect their responsibilities for tailings dam safety and be independent of production targets. The chapter also proposes that social and environmental performance staff should report up separate functional lines to the same or similar accountable executive. Many of these ideas were rejected at every opportunity by the ICMM, but some remain in the final version of the Standard. In particular, the Standard requires a so-called accountable executive, although not one who necessarily reports to the CEO. It also includes a very general requirement that bonuses for people who are responsible for tailings dam integrity and safety should reflect this fact.

The preamble to the Standard states that it embodies or seeks to embody the idea of "zero tolerance for human fatality". Chapter 9 investigates to what extent the Standard achieves this goal. It identifies 2 ways in which the Standard fails. First, it requires that dams that could kill a hundred or more, on failure, should be built to the highest of standards, while dams that could kill 1 to 10 people, on failure, may be built to lower standards. This is not consistent with the idea of zero tolerance for human fatality. The second way the Standard fails to achieve its goal is by implicitly endorsing the concept of acceptable risk, and furthermore, endorsing conventional views about what that acceptable level is. We argue that the determination of an acceptable level of risk is inherently political, and that the current credibility crisis of the industry provides a political opportunity to reduce risk to below whatever the currently acceptable levels may be.

Chapter 10 is concerned with consequence-based, as opposed to risk-based, decision-making. Suppose a mining company is trying to decide whether to build a tailings facility in a valley just above a population centre that would be obliterated if the facility failed. How should it make its decision? A purely risk-based approach to decision-making would argue as follows. Provided the facility is designed and operated to a high enough standard, the probability of failure can be made so low that the risk can be regarded as acceptable.

On the other hand, one of the undoubted achievements of the Standard is its adoption of the idea that decision making about preventing unwanted events should not be based on assessments of risk alone. It must also take account, independently, of the severity of the consequence. The ultimate implication of this view is that if the consequences of a facility failure are severe enough, then no matter how low the probability, the construction of the facility cannot be justified. The Standard does not draw this conclusion. We argue that it should have.

We have said nothing so far about how the Standard will be implemented. Chapter 11 addresses this vital question. The ICMM approach is for companies to develop their own assurance processes, using ICMM guidance. We argue that such an approach will tend to undermine the credibility of the implementation process. The better alternative is to have an independent entity, controlled by a multi-stakeholder group, that would audit against the Standard and provide certifications of compliance. It might be funded by a grant, an endowment or fees levied on companies seeking certification. An independent entity would be a natural home for the Standard, allowing for its evolution. This is the preferred alternative of the PRI and to some extent, UNEP.

Chapter 12 offers some reflections on the power of the mining industry and on the role of investors in driving change. It also laments the failure of the mining industry to learn the lessons of recent tailings dam disasters. Finally, if we are to rely on multi-stakeholder initiatives, such as the Global Tailings Review (GTR), to set new industry standards, then we should examine them closely. We therefore conclude by encouraging a greater openness to learning how multi-stakeholder initiatives function in practice.

CHAPTER 2

The Brumadinho tailings dam disaster

The Standard was intended to ensure that a disaster like Brumadinho would never occur again. That was an explicit purpose. One of the questions that can therefore be legitimately asked of the Standard is whether it would have prevented the Brumadinho failure, had Vale been in compliance with it, years earlier. For those who think this is altogether too hypothetical, we can ask the question a little differently: what are the lessons of the Brumadinho failure — lessons that need to be learnt and implemented, if future failures of this kind are to be prevented? This chapter is devoted to understanding the causes of the Brumadinho accident and therefore the lessons about what needs to be done to prevent such accidents in the future. This leads to a second important question: to what extent and in what way does the *Standard* embody the lessons from the Brumadinho disaster? We offer an answer to this question as well.

There are numerous sources available to us. One of the most useful is an inquiry report prepared at the request of Vale's board of directors.[1] The inquiry was intended to be "independent and autonomous", and to this end it was headed by a retired judge of the Brazilian Federal Supreme Court, Ellen Northfleet, who had chaired 2 previous special inquiries into corporate behaviour. The brief was to determine "causes and responsibilities" in relation to the failure. This meant that the investigation was much broader than the typical investigations commissioned by companies after major accidents, which are usually restricted to technical causes in order to avoid questions of liability.[2] The Northfleet inquiry, in contrast, covered not only the technical causes, but also the cultural and organisational causes of the accident, which made it particularly useful for our purposes. It did not seek systematically to attribute legal responsibility, but it noted that factual material relevant for the attribution of responsibility was dispersed throughout the report and it suggested that Vale should consider disciplinary action in some cases.

To make this discussion manageable, we restrict our attention to lessons that can be derived from the Northfleet report. Note that these are lessons that *we* draw from the report's analysis; they are not explicitly formulated as lessons in the report. All unreferenced material is from this source. Where we draw on other material, this is explicitly referenced.

The chapter will cover, among other things, the technical causes (very briefly), the question of how much was known beforehand about the risk of dam failure, the

---

[1] Extraordinary Independent Consulting Committee for Investigation (CIAEA), *Executive Summary of the Independent Investigation Report Failure of Dam 1 of the Córrego do Feijão Mine – Brumadinho, MG*, 20 February 2020. vale.com/PT/investors/documents/20.02.20_ciaea_report_i.pdf. Hereafter, the Northfleet report. Note that while this document is called an "executive summary", it is 45 pages in length, and no more extensive version is available in English. It is therefore reasonable to treat this as a full report.

[2] An earlier report commissioned by the company was restricted in this way. Robertson P, de Melo L, Williams D, and Ward Wilson G. *Report of the Expert Panel on the Technical Causes of the Failure of Feijão Dam I*, 12 December 2019. See also worldminetailingsfailures.org/corrego-do-feijao-tailings-failure-1-25-2019/

integrity of prior dam safety audits and the way Vale's organisational structure and its remuneration system contributed to the accident.

Geotechnical causes

For present purposes, a tailings dam can be thought of as a containment structure with a deposit of tailings behind it. The dam is periodically raised, allowing a progressively greater volume of tailings to be stored behind it. Over time, some or much of the water in the tailings drains or evaporates and the tailings deposit acquires some strength of its own. This means that it may not remain entirely reliant on the dam to hold it in place. By way of comparison, a water dam depends entirely on the dam to contain the stored water.

Under certain circumstances, a tailings deposit can suddenly lose most of its strength and behave like a liquid, putting much greater pressure on the dam. This is called liquefaction. The particular conditions under which liquefaction occurs are geotechnically complex, but the risk of liquefaction is greatest where the tailings are sand-sized, near-saturated and loose. A dam that is not designed to retain liquified tailings can fail catastrophically if liquefaction occurs. Such a dam must therefore be carefully managed, even when it is no longer receiving tailings, to ensure that conditions conducive to liquefaction do not develop or can be accommodated.

Construction of the Dam 1 at Feijão mine began in 1976 and there were 10 raises before tailings deposition ceased in 2016. The dam was not designed to withstand liquefaction, was not adequately managed and did not have adequate drainage. On 25 January 2019, following heavier than usual rain, the tailings liquified and the dam thereupon failed catastrophically.

The Lesson

Here, then, is the first lesson of the Brumandinho disaster. Dams must be designed and operated according to best engineering practice. This seems like stating the obvious. Unfortunately, it needs to be emphasised because, as the doyen of geotechnical engineers, Nobert Morgenstern has written:

> "[most tailings dam] failures arise from deficiencies in engineering practice associated with the spectrum of activities embraced by design, construction, quality control, quality assurance, and related matters. This is a very disconcerting finding".[3]

The point is that they do not fail because of extreme or unforeseeable events, or for unknown reasons. They fail because operators have not done what they should have done.

The Standard

At numerous places, the Standard requires that best engineering practices be used. If companies comply with these requirements, all will be well with respect to structural

---

[3] Morgenstern N, Geotechnical Risk, Regulation, and Public Policy, *Soils and Rocks*, São Paulo, 41(2): 107–129, May–August, 2018, p 124. This is often referred to as Morgenstern's "de Mello lecture".

integrity. What remains to be seen is how effectively compliance with the Standard will be verified.

The history of warnings and attempts to downplay them

Concern about the stability and hence the safety of the dam was expressed on numerous occasions over the life of the dam by consultants hired to conduct stability assessments:

- In 1995, the dam's safety conditions were found to be "unfavourable".

- In 2003, consultants identified an "extremely uncomfortable" situation from a risk standpoint and identified the need for a stability analysis to consider the possibility of liquefaction.

- Between 2010 and 2013, the company responsible for the dam's external audit recommended every year that analysis of the potential for liquefaction of the structure be carried out.

- Eventually, in 2014, a study of the potential for liquefaction was carried out, but no new data was collected for this study. It was based on data from 2005 that was seriously out of date, taking no account of raises that had occurred in the intervening years. Nevertheless, the study found that the dam was susceptible to liquefaction, although the likelihood of a trigger event was said to be remote.

- In 2015, the auditor recommended the collection of new data on which to base an up-to-date liquefaction study. 2015 was also the year of the Samarco failure. In response, the government decreed that all tailings dams be subject to an "extraordinary audit".

- In 2016, a study of Dam 1 was carried out for the extraordinary audit using up-to-date information, and the results were "unfavourable", indicating a situation of imminent failure. The calculations were based on best engineering practice assumptions. However, the consultant subsequently changed one of these assumptions which gave more favourable results, allowing the dam to be certified as safe.

- In early 2017, 2 other consulting companies did further stability studies that disagreed with the optimistic conclusion of the extraordinary audit. Vale's geotechnical specialists thereupon contracted another firm to develop "counter-arguments".[4]

- Later in 2017, the company responsible for the dam safety audit at the time, Tractebel, recommended in its draft report that the results of the 2016 extraordinary audit be reconsidered. However, this recommendation was deleted from the final report at the request of a Vale staff member.

It is clear from this sequence of events that there were many occasions on which the findings or preliminary findings of consultants raised concerns about the stability of the dam, findings which were largely ignored. It is also clear that Vale staff at times interacted with consultants in an effort to have unfavourable safety results changed in order to achieve safety certifications.

---

[4] Northfleet report, p 35. Subsequent page references are also to the Northfleet report.

We come now to the most recent and perhaps most notorious occasion on which the dam was certified as safe. In July 2017, the German company, Tüv Süd, was hired to perform a "periodic dam safety review". This was a 3-yearly review introduced by law after the Samarco failure of 2015. In March 2017, Vale created its own independent panel of experts to give advice on tailings facilities. The panel consisted of both national and international experts. In November 2017, this panel recommended that Vale should adopt a minimum factor of safety[5] of 1.3 in its safety reviews.[6] The precise meaning of "factor of safety" is not relevant here. What is relevant is the number itself — 1.3. Tüv Süd adopted this recommendation in the first draft of its periodic review. The actual factor of safety for Dam 1 was calculated to be 1.09. Since this was below the recommended 1.3, Tüv Süd concluded it would not be able to issue the required stability condition declaration.

There followed a series of meetings between Vale and Tüv Süd. Then, in June 2018, Tüv Süd issued the certificate. The rationale was that the factor of 1.09 was greater than 1.05, a figure cited in a journal article — an article that was not, however, intended to establish minimum factors of safety. Tüv Süd apparently agreed to sign the declaration on the basis that Vale made certain commitments to future safety improvements.

It has been alleged that Vale pressured Tüv Süd into signing the requisite certificate.[7] Since this is a matter that will ultimately be determined by the courts, we quote the Northfleet report verbatim at this point:

> "In the same period, other contracts with relevant values between Vale's Corporate Geotechnical Department and Tüv Süd were being negotiated. Messages exchanged between Tüv Süd employees at the time suggest that the perception of Tüv Süd was that it was possible that there may have been pressure on the part of Vale, including specific mention to a consulting contract that was being negotiated between Vale and Tüv Süd in the same period and actually signed thereafter."[8]

One of the Tüv Süd emails referred to in this passage read as follows:

> "... as always Vale will put us up against the wall and ask: if it doesn't pass, will you sign it or not?"[9]

The Northfleet report does not draw any explicit conclusions, but the way it is written leaves the reader with the clear impression that Tüv Süd employees felt pressured, whether or not Vale was intending to pressure them.

At a different point, the Northfleet report notes that the financial value of audit work is far less than the financial value of consulting work. It goes on:

> "The audit contracts, from a financial standpoint, were less significant than those for consulting, so they could lead companies to compromise their judgment in audits with the aim of maintaining a good relationship with Vale and entering into consulting agreements."[10]

---

[5] Peak undrained safety factor.
[6] op cit, p 21.
[7] oxebridge.com/emma/tuv-sud-auditors-arrested-claim-pressure-to-certify-doomed-brazil-dam/wsj. com/articles/brazil-police-arrest-8-vale-employees-in-dam-disaster-11550232619.
[8] op cit, p 22.
[9] wsj.com/articles/brazil-police-arrest-8-vale-employees-in-dam-disaster-11550232619.
[10] op cit, p 38, see also comment on p 42.

Following the issue of the certificate in June 2018, Tüv Süd was contracted to do the September 2018 external dam audit, a less exhaustive semi-annual audit. As noted above, an earlier audit of this type done by Tractebel had been critical of the optimistic assumptions of the extraordinary audit. The reason Vale gave for using Tüv Süd rather than Tractebel for the latest audit was a "divergence in criteria" with Tractebel.[11] Tüv Süd again certified the stability of Dam 1 on the basis of the factor safety threshold of 1.05. Again, the Northfleet report does not say so explicitly, but it invites the inference that the change of auditing company was made because at this point, Tüv Süd was more willing to bend to Vale's wishes than was Tractebel.

It remains to be said that while Vale's geotechnical departments succeeded in gaining the required certificates of stability, they were worried by the doubts being expressed by the consultants. In 2018, Vale began installing a number of "deep horizontal drains" into the dam wall in an effort to lower the water level. However, due to technical difficulties, this was abandoned, and no further efforts had been made to lower the water level before the dam failed.[12]

The lesson

The series of events described above gives rise to one of the most important lessons of the Brumadinho disaster – the need for effective policies to guard against conflicts of interest which can otherwise undermine the integrity of consultants' reports.

The Standard

In our view, the Standard does not deal adequately with this issue. It does require that:

> "The *DSR* [Dam Safety Review] contractor cannot conduct consecutive *DSRs* on the same *tailings facility* and shall certify in writing that they follow *best practices* for engineers in avoiding conflicts of interest."[13]

This requirement eliminates the potential that the contractor will provide a favourable review in order to be awarded the next review contract for the same dam. But there remains the possibility that a favourable review for the dam in question may secure a review contract for *another* dam owned by the same company. More importantly, in the light of the Brumadinho experience, there is also the possibility that a favourable review for the dam in question may secure a much more lucrative contract for other engineering services. The Standard does not deal with these possibilities explicitly, relying instead on the more general requirement that best engineering practices be followed to avoid such conflicts.

The expert panel was made aware of the conflict of interest issue at Brumadinho but failed to give it proper consideration. One member of the panel wrote an email to fellow members headed "a failure in our process", urging that the issue be given further attention. But as we shall discuss in Chapter 5, the decision-making process in the expert panel was often chaotic and the requirement wording quoted above was never debated and never revisited.

---

[11] op cit, p 20.
[12] op cit, pp 20, 25.
[13] Requirement 10.5.

The public disclosure requirements in the Standard potentially provide reassurance in this respect. However, the relevant requirement is that the operator shall publish "a summary of material findings of annual performance reviews and DSRs [Dam Safety Reviews]". Disclosure of the full reports might have provided outside parties with enough evidence to evaluate the quality and integrity of DSRs; disclosure of "a summary of material findings" is much less likely to do so.

There is an important role for governments here. Ideally, auditors could be appointed by local regulatory agencies from a list maintained for this purpose. Unfortunately, there are relatively few jurisdictions, worldwide, with the expertise and capacity to do this. Auditors selected in this way would continue to be paid by the companies. However, the expert panel could not include such requirements in the Standard because the Standard is addressed to industry and not to governments.

The knowledge of top executives

Executive managers and members of the Vale board were largely unaware of the consistently expressed concerns about the safety of Dam 1. From time to time, they received briefings about the safety of their tailings dams, but by the time information arrived at their level it had lost all detail and failed to mention significant issues. People preparing reports for upper-level managers chose simply to reassure them that all was well. For example, one presentation to upper management stated:

> "100% of Vale iron ore dams were audited in Aug 2018 and had a stability declaration issued by the external auditor with certified safety conditions. All dams are safe, stable and operate within normal range".[14]

This provides some insight into why safety certifications were so important for Dam 1. They gave the necessary assurance to upper management that all was well. Executive managers and members of the board would have had to show exceptional initiative to uncover the truth about the stability concerns that had been regularly raised about Dam 1.

Why top executives were unaware of the problems

The reason that top executives and board members were unaware of the problems with Dam 1 had much to do with Vale's organisational structure. The company was organised into autonomous business units – Iron Ore, Basic Metals, Fertilisers and Logistics. Each was a major business in its own right. In addition, there were corporate-wide functions such as internal audit, legal and compliance, but the business units minimised their dealings with these functions and operated as "silos", which the Northfleet report defined as "business units that operate in relative isolation from each other and of corporate support units".[15] In particular, the Iron Ore division consciously kept the internal audit function at arm's length. During a meeting with Vale's independent panel of experts, Iron Ore staff objected to the participation of internal audit because the meeting might include criticism of existing geotechnical risk management practices, which Iron Ore did not want to share with internal audit.[16]

14 op cit, p 32.
15 op cit, p 34.
16 op cit, p 34.

The Northfleet report notes that geotechnical and risk management services were provided by groups within the Iron Ore division. There were 2 such groups – operations geotechnical services, which managed tailings dams on a day-to-day basis, and a geotechnical risk management group, which operated at a higher level. This second group might have functioned as an expert second line of defence, overseeing the decisions of the frontline geo-technicians, except that it answered to the same Iron Ore management. In other words, it was located within the same silo and unable to operate independently of it.[17] In the words of the report, these problems "could have been minimised if there was a second line of defence for geotechnical issues that was not subordinated to the same Executive Director".[18] This line would need to have culminated in an independent executive director with accountability for geotechnical risk and the resources necessary to carry out this function.[19] As described earlier, the unfavourable reports that Vale received about the stability of Dam 1 were largely ignored, or even disputed by the geotechnical specialists within the Iron Ore division. Had they been seen by geotechnical staff within a dedicated risk management division, answerable to the CEO or even the board of the company, the outcome would likely have been different. Moreover, the external dam auditors and even the Vale panel of experts were hired by the Iron Ore geotechnical risk management group. Since these external people were also seeking to be hired to provide other services, this created a conflict of interest in which those hired had an interest in providing the advice to the risk management group that it wanted to hear.[20] No such conflict would have existed if the hiring had been done or overseen by an independent risk management function.

The lesson

Here then is another of the lessons identified in the Northfleet report. Decisions about technical risks must be overseen by a corporate risk function that bypasses the business units and is not driven by the business imperatives that operate within those units.

It appears that Vale may have subsequently implemented this lesson. It has created an executive position, answering to the CEO, entitled Executive Officer for Safety and Operational Excellence.[21] We say "may" because it is not clear from the organisational chart we have seen to what extent this position heads a function that will operate as an independent "line of defence", to use the Northfleet term, capable of intervening at the operational level. If it does have such a capacity, Vale will have taken a major step forward.

The Standard

The Standard goes some way towards implementing this lesson, but it fails to create the independent line of defence envisaged by the Northfleet report. We deal with this matter extensively in Chapter 8.

---

[17] op cit, p 36.
[18] op cit, p 41.
[19] At the corporate level, there was indeed a global business risk management group that on the face of it had some responsibility for geotechnical risk, but it lacked any technical expertise and served only as a clearing house for information received from other areas.
[20] op cit, p 41.
[21] vale.com/EN/investors/corporate-governance/Pages/default.aspx.

Risk

Historically, Vale's understanding of risk was confined to the *probability* of dam failure without considering the *consequences* of failure. The probability of failure is a technical subject that non-technical people struggle with. If senior managers are told by geotechnical engineers that the probability of failure is acceptably low according to some technical criterion, they may not be able to take the matter further. In particular, they may not feel able to raise questions about the *consequences* of a failure should one occur. This may help to explain Vale's apparent blindness to the potentially devasting consequences of failure of Dam 1. The Northfleet report made the following observation:

> "... there was a tendency towards excessive deference to the geotechnical area to deal with dam issues – understood as purely technical – to which areas other than the geotechnical area would have nothing to contribute."[22]

On the other hand, if potential consequence is taken into account, for example number of deaths that might be expected if a dam fails, other considerations can come into play and trump any arguments about probability.

Here is an example. Vale had its administration buildings located just downstream of Dam 1 and in the direct path of any tailings flow that might be released by a dam failure. These buildings at times housed hundreds of workers. An obvious way to reduce the consequence of dam failure was to relocate the administrative buildings out of harm's way. This was never considered[23] and, as it turned out, the great majority of the people killed when the dam failed were workers having lunch in these buildings. If Vale had focused on consequences of failure, and not on the assumed low probability of failure, this situation would never have been allowed to persist.

Beginning in 2018, at the prodding of Vale's independent panel of experts, the geotechnical experts employed by the company began treating risk as a product of probability times consequence. However, the Vale board was apparently not exposed to this way of thinking before the accident.[24] As a matter of fact, contemporary thinking is that consequence should be given priority over probability in decision-making about risk. We discuss this at greater length in Chapter 10.

The lesson

Decision makers need to take account of the consequences of failure independently of the probability of failure. This lesson was not explicitly stated in the Northfleet report, but it is a strong inference.

The Standard

The terms of reference for the panel required it to develop or adopt a classification of dams based on the consequences of failure. The Standard does just that, which is a significant step change. In this system of classification, Dam 1 would have

---

[22] op cit, p 39.
[23] op cit, p 40.
[24] op cit, p 39.

been described as an "extreme consequence" dam and would have been subject to the most stringent design criteria. Moreover, the Standard contains some specific references to consequence reduction in addition to risk reduction. We discuss this further in Chapter 10.

Bonuses

The Northfleet inquiry also gave consideration to Vale's bonus system – the system of variable remuneration. It found that for geotechnical staff in both the specialist areas identified above, bonuses depended largely on financial considerations. In the case of the geo-technicians responsible for day-to-day operations, there were no specific dam safety goals for 2018. For 2016 and 2017, safety goals consisted mainly of performing audits and obtaining safety certification. For the higher-level risk management group, safety goals were largely about obtaining safety certification.

In this regard, the inquiry notes that:

> "... mere regulatory compliance is rarely sufficient to guarantee the safety of highly complex structures. In the context of B1 [Dam 1], regulatory compliance ... [in particular attainment of safety certification] were prioritized, regardless of the actual safety situation of the dam."[25]

In short, for Vale, obtaining safety certification was an end in itself regardless of the real situation with respect to dam safety. The bonus system encouraged this attitude, leading ultimately to disaster.

The Lesson

Bonus systems must be carefully designed to emphasise tailings dam safety.

The Standard

This is one lesson that found its way into the Standard, although, as can be imagined, not without blood, sweat and tears – see Chapter 8. Most of the detail contained in the first drafts was eliminated, leaving it very much up to companies to decide how to implement the requirement.

Conclusion

Given that the Standard was intended to prevent further "Brumadinhos", it is appropriate to ask to what extent it incorporates the lessons of the Brumadinho disaster. Some important lessons can be extracted from the Northfleet report. This chapter has identified those lessons and made observations about the extent to which they are reflected in the Standard. We conclude that while the Standard is a big step forward, it falls short in some respects. As we observe later, there are more steps to go before we can be confident that there will be no more Brumadinhos.

---

[25] op cit, pp 34–35.

The knowledgeable reader will know that one of the lessons that the Brazilian Government drew from the Brumadinho disaster was that the method by which Dam 1 was constructed – upstream construction – is irremediably dangerous and should be banned. The Northfleet report did not address this issue. We discuss it in more detail in Chapter 5.

CHAPTER 3

A credibility crisis

The frequency and seriousness of tailings dam failures in recent decades has called into question the capacity of mining companies to operate safely. The result has been a credibility crisis for the whole industry. The global Standard is a response to this crisis.

The simplest way to demonstrate the reality of the crisis is to document the industry's own perception of the situation and the responses this has generated. The origins of the present crisis go back at least to the mid-1990s. According to the industry's peak body:

> "By the mid-to-late 1990s the mining and metals industry was in crisis. Commodity prices had plummeted, and investors were reluctant to commit to supporting mining operations. To this: growing community unrest, criticism from civil society and broader public opposition threatened industry's 'social licence to operate'. At this time of increased scrutiny, a group of industry leaders acknowledged that the sector needed to change."[1]

In response, the industry convened a massive stakeholder consultation process that culminated in 2002 with the "Toronto declaration".[2] The declaration recognised that the mining industry needed the support of the communities in which it operated and that this required serious engagement with these communities.

The enduring legacy of this crisis was the creation of the International Council of Mining and Metals (ICMM) in 2001. The mining industry is diverse, consisting of a relatively small number of global companies, hundreds of smaller mining firms and, in poorer parts of the world, thousands of very small-scale artisanal miners. The ICMM represents only the largest mining companies, 27 at the time of writing.[3] The initial aim of the Council was not simply to advance the narrowly conceived interests of the industry, but to promote sustainable development in the interests of all stakeholders. The concept of sustainable development is elaborated in a set of 10 mining principles that cover among other things, human rights, social and environmental performance, and stakeholder participation.

The Council's statement quoted above speaks of the industry's "social licence" being under threat.

It defines "social licence to operate" as follows:

> "... the ongoing approval or acceptance of a company's activities by the local community and other stakeholders. This informal endorsement can be gained and renewed through meaningful dialogue and responsible behaviour."

In this book, we speak of the industry's credibility crisis, rather than the threat to its social licence to operate. One problem with the idea of social licence is that,

---

[1] icmm.com/en-gb/about-us/annual-reviews/our-history.
[2] icmm.com/website/publications/pdfs/commitments/icmm-toronto-decleration.pdf.
[3] It also covers 36 regional and commodities associations that are not relevant for present purposes.

notwithstanding the mention of "other stakeholders" in the ICMM's definition, it is usually understood to mean a licence granted, implicitly, by the local community. The reality is the mining industry has seldom had a licence to operate in this sense. Approval has been given by governments at various levels but not by local communities, who have, at best, acquiesced to mining developments. Acquiescence is a long way from the positive approval that is suggested by the idea of a licence to operate.[4] On the other hand, credibility is not restricted to local communities but encompasses credibility in the eyes of governments and investors as well. The perceptions of this broader set of stakeholders are a vital part of the credibility crisis, as we shall shortly show.

Surprisingly perhaps, in the years immediately following the establishment of the ICMM, it was the Mining Association of Canada (MAC) rather than the International Council that appeared to take the lead in responding to the credibility crisis, driven in part by the political influence of First Nations people in Canada, supported by influential human rights and environmental organisations. We suspect it may also have been more difficult for the International Council to achieve agreement among its members than it was for the Canadian Association, whose members had a greater commonality of interests. The MAC produced a first edition of its guide to the management of tailings facilities in 1998, a second edition in 2011 and a third in 2017. It also launched a "towards sustainable mining" initiative in 2004.[5] Not surprisingly, therefore, when it came to the development of the global Standard, the Canadian mining industry and its various stakeholders were very much more influential than any other national group. Indeed, a number of the Canadian guidelines found their way into the global Standard in one way or another.

The Mount Polley tailings dam failure

Tailings facility failures continued in the years following the establishment of the ICMM at a rate of one or more per year[6] until a landmark event in 2014, the failure of the Mount Polley tailings dam in the Canadian province of British Columbia. There were no fatalities or even injuries, yet this failure caught the attention of the international community. It is worth considering why. First, it led to what was, at the time, probably the largest ever release of tailings.[7] Second, the tailings flowed into Lake Quesnel, threatening one of the largest salmon rearing grounds in Canada, and hence the cultural practices and traditional livelihoods of First Nations peoples.[8] Third, the failure happened in a country with a reputation for taking tailings dam safety more seriously than most other countries. If it could happen in Canada, it could happen anywhere. Fourth, 2 major investigations into the accident were carried out and the

---

[4] For a more extensive critique of the concept see Owen, J and Kemp, D, Social licence and mining: A critical perspective, *Resources Policy* 2012. See also dx.doi.org/10.1016/j.resourpol.2012.06.016.
    See also, Demajorovic, J, Campos Lopes, J and Frezzatti Santiago, A, The Samarco dam disaster: A grave challenge to social license to operate discourse, *Resources Policy* 2019, vol 61, pp 273–282.
[5] For information on the "Towards Sustainable Mining" initiative, see: mining.ca/towards-sustainable-mining/.
[6] See Chronology of tailings dam failures, wise-uranium.org/mdaf.html.
[7] ibid.
[8] Amnesty International, *A Breach of Human Rights: The Human Rights Impacts of the Mount Polley Mine Disaster, British Columbia, Canada*, May 2017.

reports released publicly. These identified disturbing engineering and management failures leading to the accident — failures that could easily be present in other contexts.

Samarco

Then, a year later, came the failure of the Fundão dam, operated by the Samarco company, in Brazil.[9] Samarco is a joint venture owned by 2 of the largest mining companies in the world, BHP and Vale. The Samarco failure cost 19 lives and polluted a river system all the way to the sea, nearly 900 kms away, tainting the drinking water and damaging the livelihood of hundreds of thousands of people. Samarco eclipsed Mount Polley in terms of the quantity of tailings released[10]. It has been widely described as Brazil's worst ever environmental disaster. Moreover, unlike Mount Polley, the Samarco disaster hit the world headlines over a prolonged period, significantly damaging the reputations of both Vale and BHP.

The ICMM response

The Samarco disaster, so soon after the Mount Polley failure placed the global mining industry in the spotlight, and the ICMM responded accordingly. It commissioned a report from a consulting firm, Golder, on what needed to be done. The Golder report, published in December 2016, concluded:

> "Existing published guidance and standards documentation fully embrace the knowledge required to prevent such failures. The shortcoming lies not in the state of knowledge, but rather in the efficacy with which that knowledge is applied. Therefore, efforts moving forward should focus on improved implementation and verification of controls, rather than restatement of them.
>
> It would therefore follow that a higher level of governance and assurance is required for the effective implementation of good practice."[11]

For a consultant's report, this is a remarkably forthright, indeed confronting conclusion.

In response to this challenge, in December 2016, the ICMM issued a "position statement" entitled "tailings governance framework" that contained a series of governance principles to which member companies committed themselves. The statement notes that "members are expected to implement the commitments in this position statement by November 2018".[12]

However, the statement was accompanied in small print by the disclaimer that precedes all ICMM position statements. We reproduce part of it here (with emphasis added).

> "This publication contains general guidance only... the responsibility for its adoption and application rests solely with each individual member company... Each ICMM member company is responsible for determining and implementing management practices at its facility, and ICMM expressly disclaims any responsibility related to

---

[9] "BHP Billiton 'woefully negligent' over Brazil dam collapse", BBC News, 7 May 2019.
[10] Chronology of tailings dam failures, op cit.
[11] Golder report, December 2016, p 2.
[12] icmm.com/position-statements/tailings-governance.

determination or implementation of any management practice. Moreover, although ICMM and its members are committed to an aspirational goal of zero fatalities at any mine site or facility, mining is an inherently hazardous industry, and this goal unfortunately has yet to be achieved."

The disclaimer also contains the following somewhat ambiguous statement:

"Except where explicitly stated otherwise ... this document does not constitute a position statement or other mandatory commitment that members of ICMM are obliged to adopt."

The fact is, it was entirely up to individual companies to interpret the statement as they saw fit.

The ICMM has in the past required member companies to provide some kind of assurance that they were complying with various principles and commitments, as they interpreted them. Historically, however, these assurances have been weak and unreliable. BHP was a member of the ICMM at the time of the Samarco failure, and Vale was still a member at the time of the Brumadinho failure[13]. In March 2018, a relatively new ICMM member, Newcrest, suffered a very large release at its Cadia dam in New South Wales, Australia.[14] These failures are cause for public scepticism about the effectiveness of the assurance processes in place at the time.[15]

A United Nations response

The occurrence of the Mount Polley and Samarco tailings facility failures in quick succession also triggered an intervention by the United Nations Environmental Program (UNEP). It published what it called a "rapid response assessment". The document led with the following quotation from the independent expert report on the Mount Polley failure:

"Tailings dams are complex systems that have evolved over the years. They are also unforgiving systems, in terms of the number of things that have to go right. Their reliability is contingent on consistently flawless execution in planning, in subsurface investigation, in analysis and design, in construction quality, in operational diligence, in monitoring, in regulatory actions, and in risk management at every level. All of these activities are subject to human error".[16]

Given that human error is ubiquitous, the implications for safety are clear. The only reliable solution is to phase out tailings dams in their present form and to find new technologies for dealing with mining waste. In quoting the Mount Polley report, UNEP put the industry on notice that its present technology is too dangerous to be allowed to continue.

---

[13] The owner of the Mount Polley mine, Imperial Metals, is not a member of ICMM.
[14] While the slurry was contained within the tailings facility footprint, the breach generated concern for investors, shareholders and other stakeholder groups.
[15] These assurance processes have been progressively strengthened, but they fall far short of the assurance process envisaged for the global Standard. See Chapter 11.
[16] UNEP, *Mine Tailings Storage: Safety Is No Accident: A Rapid Response Assessment* (edited by Roche, Thygesen K, Baker E), 2017, p 5.
[17] op cit, p 11.

The UNEP report then made 2 recommendations[17], the first being:

> "...safety attributes [of tailings facilities] should be evaluated separately from economic considerations, and cost should not be the determining factor."

Again, these words are taken from the expert panel report on the Mount Polley failure. They constitute a direct challenge to the dominant industry approach to safety, which is that risks must be reduced to as low as reasonably practicable. It is widely accepted in the industry that reasonable practicability includes a consideration of cost, that safety can never be evaluated independently of cost. Hence, UNEP's recommendation and the Mount Polley report on which it draws, are both asking for a revolution – a total transformation – in the way industry thinks about tailings facility safety. We can expect that the industry will continue to resist this recommendation strenuously, when the need arises.

The second recommendation is as follows:

> "Establish a UN Environment stakeholder forum to facilitate international strengthening of tailings dam regulation."

The effective implementation of this recommendation would be a blow to the mining industry since the last thing it wants is stronger state regulation. We discuss this point in more detail later.

The UNEP recommendations are a response to a loss of confidence in the ability of the mining industry to operate its tailings facilities safely. They are a manifestation of the credibility crisis the industry was experiencing.

Investor concerns

Investor groups were also concerned. Their concerns were both financial, the protection of their investments, and ethical. In particular, in 2017 the National Investing Bodies of the Church of England produced a policy document on the extractive industries that made specific mention of the safety and environmental consequence of tailings dam failures. It included the following statement.

> "We are also particularly concerned with legacy issues on disposal (i.e. sale to another owner) and closure ... [of tailings facilities. We] would support the consideration by companies of the posting of a 'tailings safety bond' and 'legacy bonds' or similar, since tailings dams appear to fail with some regularity, causing significant loss of life, and losses to communities and the environment ...
>
> Tailings bonds could act as an insurance should there be a dam burst, enabling swift access to resources by governments and impacted communities, without risk of being held up in protracted legal proceedings. They may also help focus company boards' minds on this important responsibility."[18]

This was a position that would be strenuously opposed by the ICMM when the time came, as we discuss in Chapter 6.

---

[18] Church of England Extractive Industries Policy and Advisory Papers, p 19.

But ethical investor groups went further than this.[19] The Church of England Pension Board and Sweden's Public Pension Funds wanted an independent system to verify that companies were following the highest safety standards.

They observed that the Golder report, mentioned above, had similarly recommended:

> "A tailings storage facility classification system based on the consequences of a failure, and the introduction of safety standards commensurate with the different consequence classifications."

They noted, further, that the ICMM had made no progress on this. They therefore embarked on a series of meetings with ICMM office holders and member company CEOs to promote this agenda, and they were actively engaged in this when disaster struck — again.

Investor responses to Brumadinho

The Brumadino disaster has been described as a tipping point for the industry.[20] It certainly seems to have been for the investor community. The Samarco failure had cost its owners at least $60 billion[21], and now Brumadinho would cost many billions more.

An "investor mining and tailings safety initiative" was established immediately following the failure. It was chaired by the Church of England Pensions Board and the Council on Ethics of the Swedish National Pension Fund. The Initiative was supported by 112 international investors with over US$14 trillion in assets under management. This group of investors was soon referred to as the Principles for Responsible Investment (PRI), a development that calls for some explanation.

The PRI is a United Nations-supported initiative established in 2005. It consists of a set of 6 principles to which investors are invited to sign up.[22] There are now at least 2000 signatories, and the term PRI has shifted in meaning to refer to this group of signatories. The PRI has a board and a CEO. In the tailings context, the PRI refers loosely to the 100 or more of these investors associated with the investor mining and tailings safety initiative.

Six days after the Brumadinho accident, members of this initiative (the PRI) made a public call for a new global tailings Standard to be based upon the consequences of failure. They called for the Standard to be developed independently from industry and with an emphasis on public accessibility of information about tailings. The accompanying press release read in part:

> "The [investor groups] are jointly proposing that the new system should be independent of companies and require annual audits of all tailings dams as well as verification that the highest corresponding safety standards are being implemented. All reporting should be made public through an accessible database that communities, governments, civil society and investors can access."[23]

---

[19] The following details were communicated personally.
[20] Oberle et al, *GTR Compendium*, Chapter 1, p 1.
[21] Vick, S, Dam, Safety Risk — From Deviance to Diligence, *Geo-Risk* 2017, GSP 282, p 24.
[22] unpri.org/.
[23] Church of England, *Call for new independent mine safety system to address tailings dam failures*, 31 January 2019.

This was one of the key drivers for establishing the Global Tailings Review (GTR).[24]

Some investors, including the Church of England's investing bodies, the Swedish AP Funds and Germany's Union Investments, chose almost immediately to exclude investment in Vale.[25] This decision was a clear example of what might lie in store for the mining industry if nothing changed.

However, the approach of the investor mining and safety initiative was also one of positive engagement with the industry by means of letters directly to the board, face-to-face meetings between shareholders and board members, proxy voting and the filing of shareholder resolutions (where shareholders vote or raise issues to be voted on at the Annual General Meeting).

The PRI quickly recognised that investors had very limited information about the number of tailings facilities operated by the mining companies in which they invested and about the risks associated with each facility. Its second intervention, therefore, was to request publicly listed extractive companies, 727 in total, to disclose answers to 20 questions on each tailings facility at operations they directly controlled, or where they were a joint venture partner. The questionnaire was posted online.[26]

As of March 2020, just under half of the companies approached had responded, with 152 companies confirming that they have tailings storage facilities (this includes both operator and joint venture interests). The 152 companies represent approximately 83% of the publicly listed mining industry by market capitalisation and include 45 of the 50 largest companies. Clearly, the major mining companies had taken this initiative seriously.

A third PRI intervention was the creation of a public and free-to-use global tailings data portal, ie website,[27] to make available the results of the survey. The PRI expects that this portal will also, in future, be a repository for other relevant information.

Fourth, the PRI has called for the establishment of a global independent satellite monitoring station, able to detect small movements in tailings dams before they culminate in major failures. The vision is to provide a 24/7 alert system along the lines of those established for the shipping and aviation sectors.

Finally, the PRI has suggested a need for the systematic identification and removal of the most dangerous tailings facilities, a proposal that is bound to make the industry nervous.

The PRI is clearly energised about these initiatives. According to its representatives:

> "All of these various activities are in the fascinating space where long term commercial and investor initiatives overlap with the public good – the common good. It is in society's interest to have more transparent and timely information on large structures

---

[24] GTR was the name given to the process by which the Standard was to be developed. This section draws heavily on *GTR Compendium* Chapter 16, "Investor Mining and Tailings Safety Initiative", and quotes liberally from this source, although, to save cluttering the text, quotation marks are omitted. See globaltailingsreview.org.

[25] *GTR Compendium* Chapter 16, p 217.

[26] churchofengland.org/sites/default/files/2019-04/Disclosure%20Letter%20to%20the%20Extractive%20 Industry%20.pdf.

[27] tailing.grida.no/.

that can pose risks to people and the environment. It is tragic that it takes such a catastrophe to focus minds and create the urgency that we hope can begin to make tailings facilities safer."[28]

The ICMM's commitment to an international standard

The Brumadinho tragedy was also a turning point for the ICMM. A month after the tragedy, on 26 February 2019, the ICMM made a public commitment to the establishment of a new Standard for the safer management of tailings facilities, which all its members would commit to and which non-members would be encouraged to endorse.

As described above, it had been under sustained pressure from investor groups to make such a commitment. Moreover, some of its members were outspoken on the need for this initiative. Even before it was announced, the CEO of BHP said:

> "At BHP we would welcome a common, international and independent body to oversee the integrity, construction and operation of all dams, and we absolutely support the call for increased transparency in tailings dam disclosure."[29]

Likewise, the CEO of Anglo-American backed calls for an independent third party to monitor safety of tailings dams[30]. With such public statements from its own members, it would have been difficult for the ICMM to do otherwise.

But how was this to be achieved? One possibility was for the ICMM to support the development of a tailings facility Standard to be produced by the International Standards Organisation (ISO). Some years ago, a start was made on such a Standard but it was never completed.[31] Another Standard is currently under development.[32] But neither of these standards was or is intended to cover tailings facilities throughout their life cycle, from planning to closure. Both concern closure only. There is room, therefore, for a new and comprehensive ISO Standard. However, the ISO process for formulating new standards is well established and ICMM would not have been able to control the outcome in the way it needed to do if it was going to commit its members in advance to complying with such a Standard.

Another possibility was that the ICMM might require its members to sign up to an existing international Standard, such as the Initiative for Responsible Mining Assurance. This is indeed a comprehensive Standard, but it is not focused on tailings facilities nor supported by the ICMM.

Finally, there are various national standards, notably, a guide to the management of tailings facilities, produced by the Mining Association of Canada, which should in principle have been acceptable. However, the ICMM believed non-Canadian-based companies would be reluctant to commit to such a Standard.

---

[28] Barrie S, Baker E, Howchin J and Matthews A, "Investor Mining and Tailings Safety Initiative', *GTR Compendium.*

[29] *Financial Times*, 19 February 2020, Investor groups immediately issue a press release welcoming this statement.

[30] *The Financial Times*, 21 February 2020.

[31] SO/PWI 23147, Guidelines for maintenance and monitoring of tailing storage facilities in abandoned mines.

[32] ISO 21795, Mine Closure and Reclamation Planning.

Clearly, the ICMM would need its own international Standard. However, the Standard would need to be developed through a transparent process that was independent of the industry, with input from a multi-stakeholder group, if it was to address effectively the industry's credibility crisis. As we noted earlier, in ICMM's view:

"To be a credible process it needs to be multi-stakeholder. A wholly industry-owned process will not be regarded as credible and will therefore serve no purpose."[33]

The ICMM assumption was that many of its members were already conducting themselves responsibly and that the Standard would be designed to bring poor performers into line. It would not require significant change by the good performers. There was, however, a risk that an independently created Standard might affect the interests of its members detrimentally and, as we shall see in a later chapter, much of the ICMM's energy was directed at ensuring that this did not happen.

Having found itself with little option but to commit to a new Standard, the ICMM now took the initiative in developing the organisational machinery by which it would be constructed. The Standard would be drafted by a group of experts, and would have 3 co-conveners, who would all need to approve it.[34] The ICMM would be one of those conveners, which would enable it to exercise a veto, if that should ever prove necessary. The second obvious convener was the PRI, which had already called for such a Standard. And the third was UNEP, which had previously recommended stronger international regulation. An international Standard, backed by appropriate incentives to comply, would certainly amount to stronger international regulation, albeit by the private sector, not the state. PRI and UNEP could be expected to act as a counterweight to the ICMM to ensure that the Standard represented the interests, not only of the mining companies but also of communities and environments affected by tailings facilities, as well as the interests of investors.

Apart from jointly approving the final Standard, the co-conveners would jointly determine the process by which the Standard was drafted, and they would jointly select an independent chair of the drafting panel. The chair would select the expert panel to assist with the drafting of the Standard. We describe the composition of this panel in Chapter 5.

The co-conveners also decided that an advisory group would act as a sounding board for the panel chair and expert panel, and provide feedback on drafts of the Standard. It would consist of representatives of non-governmental organisations (NGOs), finance interests, geotechnical specialists and others.

As it turned out, there was only one person on the advisory group representing local communities directly affected by a tailings facility failure – Jacinda Mack, a member of the Xat'sull (Soda Creek) First Nation from Canada. Jacinda Mack's public advocacy work gave the panel insight into the impact of a tailings facility failure on Indigenous peoples. In describing the Mount Polley disaster, she said:

"It was a shock. All the communities around there when that happened had an emergency meeting. People were crying and talking about it like there had been a death. We did a ceremony there on the banks of the Quesnel River in Likely. We

---

[33] See Appendix 1.
[34] *ICMM, UN Environment Programme and Principles for Responsible Investment agree to co-convene mine tailings storage facilities review*, ICMM Press Release, 27 March 2019.

did a ceremony you do in a time of grief, of great loss and that's exactly how our communities were all feeling".[35]

Even though lives were not lost in the Mount Polley failure, the damage to places of cultural and ecological significance, and the associated loss and trauma from this event was catastrophic for First Nations people. Unfortunately, a failure without fatalities could not be classified as "catastrophic" within the framework that had been established for the creation of the Standard. We say more about this later.

Finally, there was no voice on the advisory group representing tailings facility workers, although representatives had been invited. This was a serious gap, given that the great majority of the people killed in the Brumadinho accident were working on site.

There was one other aspect of the expert panel's work that consumed a great deal of the time and energy. A draft of the Standard served as the basis of an extensive public consultation process in which people and organisations were able to make written submissions or attend meetings at various locations around the world where they could provide oral feedback. This feedback was compiled and uploaded to the GTR website, alongside the expert panel's responses. In this way, the GTR provided a certain level of transparency and public accountability. We mention this here for completeness given our focus on those parts of the GTR that were more hidden from public view. However, the consultation process itself will not feature prominently in our account.[36]

This elaborate organisational machinery was intended to provide as much credibility as possible to the Standard that finally emerged.

Explaining the ICMM commitment to an international standard

With the Mount Polley disaster, followed in quick succession by the 2 tailings dam disasters in Brazil, the credibility of the industry was at rock bottom. As one investor representative said: "We have lost confidence in the sector's ability to regulate itself on this issue."[37] This was a matter of great concern to the mining industry for various reasons; we mention 2 here.

The first was that major accidents are often followed by tougher regulation, particularly in the states, provinces or territories in which the accident occurred. In the state of Minas Gerais in Brazil, in which both the Samarco and Brumadinho disasters occurred, legislation now bans the construction of new dams if there are settlements within 10 kms downstream, or if there is a possibility that a tailings flood might reach a community in less than 30 minutes. The distance can be increased

---

[35] thenarwhal.ca/jacinda-mack-wants-to-get-real-about-what-that-mine-is-actually-going-to-do-to-your-community/.

[36] For more information on this process, see *Global Tailings Review Consultation Report*, August 2020. globaltailingsreview.org.

[37] Church of England, *Call for new independent mine safety system to address tailings dam failures*, Church of England media release, 31 January 2020.

to 25 kms in certain circumstances.[38] Moreover, since the Brumadinho disaster, the construction of so-called upstream dams has been banned in Brazil. This kind of legislative response is anathema to ICMM members.

The current credibility crisis raises the possibility that more states may take such actions, as NGOs are demanding.[39] Such bans could easily be extended to prohibit other kinds of tailings disposal currently in use, such as riverine disposal, dumping tailings into river systems, as happens in some parts of the world (see Chapter 6). These are very real threats that the industry wishes to avoid. The ICMM commitment to a global industry Standard, was in part intended to forestall such prohibitions.

A second reason for the ICMM's decision to commit to a Standard was concern about the reaction of investors. Investor activism has been growing for years in relation to climate change risks. There was, from the industry point of view, a risk that investors might react to the unfolding credibility crisis of the mining industry in a similar way, choosing not to invest in some companies or even to divest. We have already noted that following Brumadinho the PRI launched a disclosure request to the industry designed to provide investors with better information on which to base investment decisions. We noted, too, that the threat to divest has become a reality, with some investors withdrawing from Vale. From an industry point of view, these are disturbing developments. A Standard that had the imprimatur of the PRI might counteract this threat. This would be most effective if the PRI were willing to accept some form of certification against the Standard as a demonstration that tailings risks were adequately under control. This issue of certification is therefore critical; we address it in detail in Chapter 11.

In summary, the credibility crisis of recent years was not just a temporary problem that would be followed by a return to business as usual. It threatened permanent changes detrimental to the interests of the mining industry. The Standard represented a way of forestalling these changes.

However, from the ICMM's point of view, the development of the Standard would be a balancing act. The industry would need to relinquish some degree of control over how it did business, while at the same time protecting its fundamental interests. How this was done is the subject of the next chapter.

---

[38] Earthworks and Mining Watch Canada, *Safety First: Guideline for Responsible Mine Tailings Management*, June 2020, pp 11–12.
[39] ibid.

CHAPTER 4

The influence of the ICMM on the construction of the Standard

The process by which the Standard was constructed was based on 2 foundational principles. The first was that the International Council of Mining and Metals (ICMM) was one of 3 equal, co-convening parties, the other 2 parties being the Principles for Responsible Investment (PRI) and the United Nations Environment Program (UNEP). The documents that established the review specified that these parties would have "equal say", and key decisions about the process would need to be by "mutual agreement". It also specified that the output of the review – the Standard – "must enjoy the support of the three co-conveners" (see Appendix 1).

The second principle was that the review process was to be "independent". This word was used repeatedly in the Global Tailings Review (GTR) foundational documents, but its meaning was never clarified.

In this chapter, we show that in practice the co-conveners were far from equal and that the ICMM wielded much greater influence than the other 2. Some rebalancing of relative influence occurred towards the end of the process, but the dominance of the ICMM was never in doubt. We also show that the process by which the Standard was constructed was not and could never have been truly independent.

This is not to say that the Standard is one that the industry would have come up with by itself. Far from it. There are many features of the Standard that are novel from an industry point of view, and many that involved considerable compromise for industry participants. But during the development of the Standard, industry retained for itself a power of veto, which it exercised in various ways when it felt its fundamental interests were at stake. Neither of the other co-conveners was able to exercise such power, except for one occasion towards the end of the negotiations when UNEP threatened to withdraw from the process. This chapter will demonstrate these claims in some detail and will also offer some insights into why events unfolded in this way.

The following narrative is not intended to be a complete account of the process. In particular, we barely mention the advisory group that had input into the process, and we provide no account of the public consultations in which we received input from interested parties around the world. The focus here is on the relative influence of the 3 co-conveners and on the extent to which the expert panel was able to work independently.

We stress, too, that the process did not unfold according to a pre-determined plan. It was to some extent made up on the run and was quite chaotic at times. No one foresaw, for example, that there would be 5 iterations of the draft before one was ready to be presented to the co-conveners for their consideration and endorsement.

Finally, to understand the role played by the ICMM, it will be helpful to bear in mind that it is a Council of member companies, represented by their CEOs. It employs a secretariat, headed by a chief executive officer and chief operating officer, but this secretariat must seek authorisation from the Council for all significant decisions. In particular, the Council CEOs were closely involved in the delivery of ICMM feedback on the various drafts of the Standard.

An asymmetric starting point

The GTR was an expensive undertaking, costing many millions of dollars. ICMM member companies paid all these costs, neither the PRI nor UNEP contributed. Furthermore, members of the expert panel and the administrative staff for the review signed contracts with the ICMM, not with the chair of the review. Various clauses in the contracts specified that the ICMM would retain ownership of the products. These clauses had few practical consequences, but they did serve to underline that panel members had legal obligations to the ICMM with no similar obligations to the other 2 co-conveners. This was indeed an asymmetric starting point.

The terms of reference

The terms of reference agreed by the co-conveners were broad. However, there were some matters that were explicitly stated to be beyond the scope of the review. In particular:

> "The review will not look to exclude certain technologies such as upstream tailings storage facilities from future use."

This requirement reflected the interests of ICMM members, as we shall discuss in more detail in Chapter 6.

However, the PRI wrote in its later submission to the panel that there is a:

> "... possibility that some types of dam are too risky in certain circumstances. **If the review considers this to be the case, even if it is a very remote possibility that an operator would build such a facility, this ought to be articulated. E.g. Upstream dams are unsuitable for areas subject to prolonged high rainfall and seismic activity".** (Emphasis in original.)

On one interpretation, this statement contradicts the prohibition in the terms of reference. But even if it is not strictly contradictory, it is clear that the PRI would not at its own initiative have declared at the outset that a prohibition of certain technologies was beyond scope. The existence of this limitation of scope demonstrates the way in which the ICMM sought to influence the agenda from the outset.

A preliminary skirmish

Well before our process had begun, the ICMM had already convened a working group of tailings experts from among its member companies to develop an "international guide for tailings management". One of the stated aims of this guide was to "provide comprehensive guidance on principles and practices for tailings management".[1] This

---

[1] ICMM Guidance Document Subgroup, *Input on Global Tailings Review Draft Standard*, 30 August 2019, p 1.

was precisely the task of the expert panel, and seemed to the panel at best redundant and at worst an attempt to influence it in ways that were not open to the other 2 co-conveners at that time.

A second and more limited objective of the group was to support "implementation of the international Standard for tailings management", which the expert panel was to develop. However, this objective was premature because the GTR was later to sketch an implementation process that was quite independent of the ICMM (see Chapter 11).

In a written submission based on the first, limited circulation draft of the global Standard, the ICMM group wrote:

> "There is no reference [in the draft Standard] to the international guide to tailings management being developed by the ICMM, the Standard should refer to the Guide."[2]

And again:

> "There is an expectation of alignment between the Standard and the guidance document, but given the current content of the Standard, alignment will be difficult to achieve."[3]

Clearly, the view of the ICMM was that the Standard should be adjusted to bring it into line with the ICMM guide.

At an early stage in the process, the expert panel met with representatives of this ICMM group to try to understand this confused and contradictory situation, but the meeting failed to achieve any clarity. Fortunately, the group suspended its activities until after the Standard might appear, at which time its role could be expected to become clearer. But the very existence of this group and its expectation that the panel would incorporate its views into the Standard was an early indication of the pressure the ICMM would bring to bear.

An initial powerplay

The expert panel's first major goal was to construct a preliminary draft of the Standard for public consultation. This was to be translated into several languages to ensure the widest possible input. Interested parties, including the 3 co-conveners, were to be invited to make formal submissions, based on this draft. As a matter of courtesy, the chair of the panel provided advance copies to the co-conveners. The ICMM distributed this draft to the CEOs of its 27 member companies for comment and received very strong objections to some of the provisions in the draft. As a result, the ICMM "red lined" these provisions, insisting they be changed before the ICMM CEOs would agree that the draft be sent out for consultation. The other 2 co-conveners were not prepared to express a view at this stage and took the position that they would endorse whatever the panel chair decided. Part of their reason for this was their view that to intervene more forcefully would undermine the independence of the expert panel. Furthermore, the PRI took the view that it was not sufficiently knowledgeable about the issues to debate the details. What it wanted was a Standard that would prevent another Brumadinho from occurring, and it was relying on the independence of the expert panel to deliver such a Standard. Neither

---

[2] op cit, p 10.
[3] op cit, p 2.

UNEP nor the PRI recognised that, paradoxically, their intervention would have given the panel chair greater room to exercise the independence they so valued.

The non-intervention of UNEP and the PRI left the panel chair in a weak position and he was forced to concede to some of the demands of the ICMM CEOs in order to keep the process going. So the version that went out to public consultation was already modified to take account of some of the ICMM's objections without any countervailing input from the other 2 co-conveners.

There had been no need for intervention by the ICMM CEOs at this stage. They were not approving the consultation draft, and there was plenty of opportunity to express their views in a submission during the consultation stage. Moreover, as a result of this intervention, the public was denied access to the considered views of the expert panel on certain matters. We shall elaborate on some of these substantive issues later in this book; here, we are talking only about the process.

The advisory group was made privy to ICMM's intervention and the resultant changes to the draft, and many of its members were horrified. They regarded this as undue interference and saw it as undermining the independence of the process.

The ICMM intervention was also a crisis for the expert panel. Some members felt that their independence and even their integrity had been compromised and briefly considered resigning. In the end, however, they were persuaded that there would be opportunities to recover some of what had been deleted and that all was not lost.

As for the ICMM itself, some of its representatives later conceded that the intervention had been a mistake. However, after the Standard was launched, the incoming chair of the ICMM's Council of CEOs described the intervention as:

> "[the way in which the ICMM] regained the initiative on the tailings Standard effort following receipt ... of the unacceptable draft Standard planned for distribution for public comment by the co-conveners ... [This was] a good outcome ... It required hard work and commitment. Success always does".[4]

The submissions by the co-conveners

Following the publication of the consultation draft, numerous submissions were received from a wide range of interested parties as well as from the co-conveners. We comment here only on the latter, since these were the submissions the expert panel needed to attend to most carefully.

For the first time, the panel now had some clear input from the PRI and UNEP as well as the ICMM. However, in the covering letter accompanying its submission, the ICMM made the following statement.

> "The ICMM members, as the builders and operators of tailings storage facilities, have the most critical vested interest of the three co-conveners in achieving our shared aim of the development of an international Standard for the safer management of tailings facilities that is fit for purpose."

---

[4]   Memo from Richard Adkerson, 9 September 2020.

This is certainly a debatable proposition, but we shall not pause to debate it now. The point we wish to emphasise is that it is a thinly disguised request by the ICMM to the expert panel to give priority to its views, ahead of those of the other 2 co-conveners. In so saying, the ICMM is departing from the principle of equality among the co-conveners, which was so important to the credibility of the Standard.

There is also a clear threat of veto contained in the covering letter:

> "Our view is that there are some very substantive core issues to be addressed before the ICMM will be able to endorse the final Standard."

It was obvious from the submissions that the ICMM and its member companies had been able to deploy far more resources in preparing its submission than had the other 2 co-conveners. The ICMM made detailed track changes to many of the Standard's 70 odd requirements and they provided a detailed standalone document justifying each of these changes. Generally speaking, the other 2 co-conveners did not respond in such detail.

In particular, although the PRI consulted widely with its members, its submission did not request specific changes to the draft in the way that the ICMM's submission did. Here is what the PRI said about its submission.

> "The following comments are on the whole high-level that are appropriate to the role that the PRI has sought to play in this process. We have been happy to include some more technical comments from some investors in this submission, these being comments from investors with in-depth technical expertise in mining. In some cases, these investors have made their own submissions to the Consultation."[5]

The submission passes on these "technical comments" without specifically endorsing them. These comments therefore do not constitute requests made by the PRI. As a result, there is very little in the submission that might serve to counterbalance the ICMM's threat of veto.

The UNEP submission, in contrast, had some very clear "should" statements that contradicted some of the ICMM's requirements. These were described as having "fundamental importance", but they were not described as prerequisites that would need to be met to secure UNEP endorsement of the Standard. Here is one example. It is based on the principle that, where a tailings facility failure could have catastrophic consequences, the construction or operation of the facility needed approval from the highest level of the organisation. The pre-consultation draft of the Standard specified that where the failure of a proposed new tailings facility could cause large numbers of fatalities:

> "the board shall be responsible for approving the proposal".

This was one of the matters the CEOs had objected to. They had changed it in the consultation draft to a requirement that:

> "the board *or senior management (as appropriate, based on the Operator's organisational structure)* shall be responsible for approving the proposal...". (Emphasis added.)

5   Matthews, ACT and Howchin, J, *Global Tailings Review Consultation Submission From UN-Backed Principles for Responsible Investment (PRI) Co-Convenors*, 31 December 2019, p 4. globaltailingsreview. org/wp-content/uploads/2020/07/Principles-for-Responsible-Investment-response.pdf.

UNEP responded to this in its submission as follows:

> "The Standard should clearly point to the fact that the Board has responsibility for tailings facilities and accountability for their failures. The current reference to the highest level decision maker being a senior manager is unacceptable. While a senior manager could be involved in day-to-day follow-up and activities, responsibility should remain with the Board."

This contradicted the ICMM position. Importantly, the contradiction provided a space in which the expert panel could work to fashion a compromise solution. From early in the process, the panel had hoped that the conveners would specify their points of disagreement in this way, so that it could work towards mutually acceptable solutions. However, things seldom worked out in this way. In particular, the panel feared it would be unable to respond effectively to some of UNEP's statements of "fundamental importance" because of the threatened ICMM veto.

As a next step in the process, the panel chair arranged for the 3 co-conveners to speak separately to the panel about their submissions and to answer questions. These were not intended to be negotiating sessions in which the participants would seek to come to agreements. Rather, they were information gathering exercises. The panel's major aim was to clarify exactly how much room to move it had in constructing the next draft without triggering a veto that might make the process unravel. Both the PRI and UNEP met with the panel for about 2 hours in teleconferences. Neither presented the panel with any non-negotiable demands.

The ICMM's approach to its session was quite different. The expert panel was due to meet in Brisbane, and the ICMM asked to join the panel for a day-long session. It sent a 6-person negotiating team, headed by one of the mining company CEOs on the Council. On the day of the meeting, the ICMM team expected to go through their submission and resolve points of disagreement, one by one. Their view was that if the ICMM was able to negotiate an agreed text with the expert panel, there would be no need for a final meeting of the 3 co-conveners. They were visibly shocked when the chair made it clear that the panel did not intend to reach an agreed version on the spot, but would develop the next draft at a later time, taking account of the comments of all 3 co-conveners, as well as the submissions and comments made by other interested parties during the consultation period. The chair explained again that in the final analysis the ICMM would need to negotiate with the other co-conveners to reach a mutually agreed version. The ICMM negotiating team caucused at least once behind closed doors to deal with this new realisation.

Despite the strong position adopted by the panel chair at this meeting, some members of the expert panel had been intimidated by the ICMM. In subsequent discussions within panel, there was talk of the need to avoid provoking the ICMM, where possible, and pressure was put on some panel members to relinquish certain positions they had espoused. We say more about these internal workings of the panel in a later chapter. But the point here is that, in the absence of countervailing pressure from UNEP or the PRI, the panel felt impelled to concede on some matters.

Subsequent drafts

It was hoped that the next draft produced by the expert panel would be the last and that it would then be over to the co-conveners to negotiate a final text. However, things did not work out that way. A series of meetings was arranged, to be held in Stellenbosch, near Cape Town, South Africa, in January 2020. The venue was chosen because many participants were expected to be in Cape Town for a mining investment conference, the African Mining Indaba. It was expected that the much-awaited meeting of the co-conveners to deal with remaining points of disagreement would take place here. To this end, the chair circulated a "provisional" post-consultation draft a few days before the Stellenbosch meetings. The PRI and UNEP both took the view that they did not have sufficient time to consider the latest draft and cancelled their attendance.

However, ICMM representatives were there in considerable numbers and met with the expert panel for 2 half-day sessions. At the first of these meetings, the ICMM again urged that the panel should negotiate with it directly, on the detail. It also expressed the hope that members of the expert panel would be able to publicly endorse the Standard, since in the end "everyone would agree". The ICMM again seemed surprised when the panel said it did not intend to agree to the requested changes on the spot, and the representatives again found it necessary to caucus separately when this became apparent.

At the second meeting with the ICMM, the next day, the panel was addressed by another of the Council's mining company CEOs who stressed that the ICMM was looking for solutions that would be acceptable to boards and senior management. The Stellenbosch meetings thus turned out to be another opportunity for the ICMM to press its case without any countervailing pressure from UNEP or the PRI.

A week later, UNEP and the PRI were ready to provide their comments on the post-consultation draft. An arrangement was made to meet in Zürich, the most convenient location for attendees. The ICMM was again present, at the request of UNEP, so this was the first time all 3 co-conveners met together with the panel. Discussion was robust and there remained points of disagreement among the co-conveners. The chair's view at this stage of the process was that expert panel members were "facilitators, not holders of interest". This was a convenient posture aimed at moving the process forward as expeditiously as possible. But for panel members selected for their expertise, this was an uncomfortable situation to find themselves in. The panel subsequently produced its final draft, reflecting the discussion, which was sent to the co-conveners to agree on a final version. The expert panel was not present for this ultimate negotiation between the co-conveners and had no part in the final shaping of the Standard.[6]

The co-convener negotiations

The final negotiations of the co-conveners were more protracted than was originally envisaged, taking place over a period of weeks via Zoom conferences and telephone calls. The ICMM had the largest negotiating contingent, consisting of 2 ICMM officer bearers and 6 company CEOs. UNEP also brought more people to the table

---

[6] The panel was afforded the opportunity to review the final version before its release.

and became more assertive than it had previously been. Finally, the role of the PRI shifted subtly. It adopted a mediator role between the ICMM and UNEP, at one stage tabling 7 draft options for one requirement in an effort to find an acceptable compromise.

But despite UNEP's newfound assertiveness, the imbalance identified earlier remained. This is perhaps symbolised by the ICMM's description of the points it brought to the table as "redline issues", while UNEP described its points only as "key messages".

In fact, the ICMM prevailed on the issues it regarded as critical. For instance, the draft Standard developed by the panel contained requirements that companies be able to certify that they had the resources to close tailings facilities at the end of their life cycle, and that they be insured against catastrophic failure. The ICMM declared these provisions unacceptable, as worded, and they were substantially weakened. We discuss this in more detail in Chapter 6.

Another matter on which the ICMM prevailed concerned the issue of public disclosure. The panel's draft Standard required that companies make public their inundation maps, that is, the areas that could be impacted in the event of a dam failure. This was a matter on which both UNEP and the PRI felt strongly. However, the ICMM argued that this could be counterproductive. UNEP pointed out that in the oil and gas industries, as well as the nuclear industry, companies were required to make public the areas that would be affected in the event of a catastrophic spill or release. But in the end, this public disclosure requirement was deleted. In its place companies were to provide "sufficient information" to local authorities and emergency services to enable disaster management planning. This was a significant step back from *public* disclosure of the *area that would be inundated* by a tailings dam failure.

There was one substantive matter on which UNEP prevailed. It did so because of a particular event that sent shock waves through the mining industry just at the time the co-conveners were finalising the Standard. The mining company, Rio Tinto, used explosives to expand a mine site in the vicinity of Juukan Gorge in northern Australia. It did so, knowing that this would destroy ancient caves that contained aboriginal artefacts and evidence of human habitation dating back 46,000 years. The company destroyed the caves with the approval of the Western Australian Government, but against the wishes of the traditional owners of the land.

Requirement 1.2 in the final Standard concerns the prior consent of indigenous peoples for new tailings facilities. During final negotiations, and just prior to the destruction of the Juukan Gorge caves, the ICMM had succeeded in adding the following sentence to the requirement.

> "An Operator applying the ICMM Position Statement on Indigenous Peoples and Mining will be considered to meet this Requirement."

Clearly, the ICMM's position statement had not prevented Rio Tinto from destroying the Juukan Gorge caves. This strengthened UNEP's resolve to reject the ICMM addition, and it threatened to withdraw from the process altogether unless the ICMM addition was removed. The subsequent negotiations were intense, and a form of wording was eventually agreed that left it ambiguous as to whether compliance with the ICMM position statement would satisfy the Standard. On the face of it, UNEP had exercised its power of veto effectively, but in the final analysis it is not clear how much the ICMM had given up. The full implications of the destruction of the Juukan Gorge caves will be addressed in Chapter 7.

Summary

The principle that the co-conveners would have equal say was not upheld. The ICMM consistently argued that its views should take precedence over those of the other 2, and it backed this up throughout the development of the Standard with an implied threat that it would bring the process to a halt if its fundamental interests were disregarded. Moreover, the ICMM was able to bring far more resources to bear in its efforts to influence the expert panel. This might not have mattered if the expert panel had been truly independent, but it was not. It was the 3 co-conveners who would together agree on a final version. The expert panel did not have the final say. Its job was to find a way to reconcile the conflicting demands and interests of the co-conveners, as far as possible. This meant that it had to pay greatest attention to the most influential voice − that of the ICMM. The panel was engaged in a political process. It was not tasked with authoring the Standard itself. Instead its task was to produce a draft that stood the best chance of being approved by the 3 co-conveners. To repeat, this does not mean that the Standard is a sham. Not at all. It is a major advance on what has gone before. But the multi-stakeholder process by which it was developed was far more lop-sided than envisaged in the original documentation.

CHAPTER 5

The functioning of the expert panel

We are sometimes asked how the expert panel operated and how it made decisions. Small group decision-making is inevitably problematic, so these are indeed questions worth exploring. We do not intend to devote a lot of attention to this issue. But it is a sufficiently self-contained topic to constitute a separate chapter, albeit a small one.

All of what is known about small group decision-making was in evidence in this case. In large groups, decisions can be made by voting with the majority view prevailing. Dissenting views are not suppressed; they are simply outvoted. But in small groups, the situation is different. Small groups tend to develop some degree of group solidarity, and a decision-making process that leaves an unresolved difference of opinion can be socially divisive. Accordingly, in small groups, decisions are expected to be made by consensus and it is implicitly assumed that the group decision can and will be unanimous. This results in the suppression of dissenting views and prevalence of "group think", which can sometimes lead to disastrous outcomes.

An outstanding example of this pressure to conform is provided by the launch of the *Challenger* space shuttle in 1986. The shuttle caught fire soon after take-off and 7 astronauts died.[1]

The anticipated air temperature at the time of launch was lower than it had ever been, creating significant doubts among engineers about the wisdom of the launch. A group of 4 managers was required to make the decision. Within the group, 3 favoured authorising the launch, while the fourth, an engineer, wavered. The senior manager in the group asked the waverer "to take off his engineering hat and put on his management hat", after which he agreed to go along with the majority view. The launch decision could therefore be portrayed as unanimous.

We do not suggest that the expert panel was making life and death decisions, as in the *Challenger* case, but the *Challenger* incident does highlight the problematic nature of consensus decision-making in any small group. It was to be expected, therefore, that the decision-making process of the expert panel would be problematic.

Consider first the composition of the panel. It consisted of:

- a chair, with long experience in running government, semi-government and non-government environmental organisations, but no previous connections with the mining industry

- 2 geotechnical engineers with long careers as consultants in tailings facility engineering

- 2 sociologists with specialist knowledge of the social impact of mining on local communities, one an academic (Kemp) and one a consultant

---

[1] Vaughan, D, *The Challenger Launch Decision*, Chicago: University of Chicago Press 1997, pp 316–318.

- one academic sociologist with specialist knowledge of the organisational causes of major accidents in the resources sector (Hopkins)

- one consultant with specialist knowledge of the environmental impact of mining, and

- one academic lawyer with a special focus on environmental protection law.

This is obviously not a group of industry insiders. Admittedly, some panel members made their living by working for mining companies, and some others engaged in industry-sponsored research. On the other hand, the professional reputations of these individuals depended on their willingness to provide independent, uncompromised advice to the companies to whom they consulted.

Although there were 3 sociologists on the panel, they did not constitute a disciplinary grouping, since organisational behaviour and the social performance of mining companies are very different sub-disciplinary areas of sociology. If there was any other affinity grouping on the panel, it was the 4 people whose interests, collectively, were in the social and environmental performance of the mining industry.

This was a panel with wide-ranging expertise. It is not a panel that the industry itself might have been expected to assemble. It boded well for the credibility of the Standard.

Panel members knew little about each other and each other's expertise. How was such a disparate group going to be able to work together effectively? At the outset, the chair asked one of the geotechnical engineers to make a presentation on the problem of tailings facilities and what some of the potential issues might be. In retrospect, it would have been desirable if each member had been given the opportunity to present their disciplinary perspective on the problem and to explain how they might be able to contribute to the Standard. This did not happen and the non-engineers in the group felt at a distinct disadvantage. Each panel member was asked to propose specific requirements for the Standard, but there was never time to elaborate on their importance, which was often not appreciated fully by the others. For example, in talking about organisational issues, it was critical to have a clear understanding of the meaning of "operator" and the significance of "joint venture" as an organisational form. Even towards the end of the process, these things were not fully understood. Indeed, it was only after the expert panel had largely finished its work that the authors of this book had a chance to read some of each other's work and to understand the full importance of what the other had been saying during the panel deliberations.

The process was to propose requirements for the Standard in individual areas of expertise or interest and then collectively to critique these proposals. At times, this was quite unruly. The chair did not initially control meetings in a rigid way. He took the view that the panel members were the experts and it was up to them to settle the details. But there was no strategy for settling disagreements and some matters were revisited on several occasions without coming to a resolution. Often, panel members interrupted each other without listening or trying to understand what the other was saying, and at times meetings were extremely tense. On more than one occasion someone left the room in tears or ended up feeling so frustrated or disrespected that they could not participate in after-work socialising. In the end, the person in whose area of expertise the matter ostensibly lay was often left to "hold the pen" and finalise the wording of a requirement. This left those with contrary, but often quite legitimate views, in a weaker position.

Occasional group activities were arranged so that the chair and panel members had an opportunity to "decompress" after intense exchanges. Mostly, people participated, recognising the importance of maintaining collegial relations.

One philosophical division in the panel tended to be enduring. On one hand, some felt that a draft was needed that truly embodied the ideal of safety first, realising that the co-conveners would then need to modify it in order to achieve agreement. On the other hand, others felt that the panel needed to be "realistic", that is, to produce a document there was some chance industry would accept. Over time, given the unequal pressures being applied by the co-conveners, this tension was resolved more and more in favour of "realism".

Into this cauldron went the input from the advisory panel and from the public consultation process. Where input was non-controversial, it was easy enough to incorporate. But given the diverse backgrounds of the members of the advisory panel and wide spectrum of parties who made submissions, it was inevitable that much of this input would be contradictory and therefore not readily assimilable. Individual contributions were useful in supporting various sides of various ongoing debates within the expert panel, but many of those who made submissions, and particularly members of the advisory panel, would have felt, understandably, that the expert panel had paid very little attention to their input.

Part way through the process and at the panel's request, the chair began to play a more decisive role. He was an advocate for the "realistic" approach. He stressed that the panel was involved in a political process in which it was better to achieve something, rather than nothing. It was here that the group pressures became intense, compelling some members to give up on certain matters for the sake of achieving an elusive consensus. Every member of the panel was occasionally forced to give ground in this way.

Out of this messy process came the final draft sent to the co-conveners for their deliberations. Doubts or reservations had been silenced, but to describe it as a consensus document hides a far more fractured reality. The draft was the outcome of a political process and not something everyone was happy with. Nevertheless, it was a considerable achievement that, if implemented, could be expected to reduce the risk of future tailings facility failures. This question of implementation will be taken up in Chapter 11.

CHAPTER 6

The scope of the Standard

Civil society organisations criticised the panel for failing to take a stand on some important issues. By contrast, industry organisations criticised the panel for straying too far from the agreed task. They insisted that certain matters were "out of scope". For instance, a covering letter to one of the International Council on Mining and Metals (ICMM) submissions said bluntly:

> "We request you ... to ensure that the development of the Standard remains centred and focussed on its original purpose and intent. We hope that you will thereby avoid any creep in scope or content".

In this chapter we outline some of the ways in which scope was contested, and to what effect.

We deal to varying degrees with 5 sets of issues:

- Matters clearly specified as out of scope in the foundation document for the Global Tailings Review (GTR).
- Acute versus chronic failures.
- Financial assurance and insurance.
- Governance arrangements.
- The rights of affected communities.

The initial scope of the GTR was outlined in a document that described the process for the Standard's development (see Appendix 1). No explicit terms of reference were included. The documentation nonetheless specified a number of matters that should be considered as part of developing the Standard. It also stated that, while the Standard was "not limited to" these matters, certain matters were "beyond the scope of the present review". Specifically:

- "The review will not look to exclude certain technologies such as upstream tailings facilities from future use".
- "Riverine, deep sea and non-tailings related storage of materials will not be included in this review".
- "Standards for rehabilitation of affected areas will not be part of the review".

These are unambiguous limitations to the scope of the Standard. On agreeing to participate in the process, panel members had little option but to comply. As we noted in Chapter 4, these restrictions were included at the behest of the ICMM, not the Principles for Responsible Investment (PRI) or the United Nations Environment Program (UNEP), although of course they acquiesced. The full significance of these restrictions may not be apparent to the reader. In following sections, we delve into 2 of them:

- The instruction not to ban the method of upstream dam construction.
- The instruction not to consider riverine disposal of tailings.

A ban on upstream construction?

Some of the best-known tailings facility failures of recent years have involved the so-called upstream construction method. Consequently, many stakeholders argue that this construction method should be banned. For example, 2 prominent groups, Earthworks and Mining Watch Canada, have urged that:

> "The use of upstream dams must be banned in favor of centerline and downstream dams, which are much less vulnerable to all mechanisms of dam failure".[1]

Upstream dam construction is already banned in several countries in South America, including Brazil, after its 2 recent disasters.

To understand this issue requires some additional background. A tailings facility is constructed by building a starter dyke or embankment across a valley,[2] using earth and rock. (See starter dyke 1 in the top panel in Figure 6.1.) Tailings, in the form of a slurry, are then piped in upstream of the dam wall, until the dam is almost full. In the upstream method, dyke 2 is then constructed, slightly upstream of dyke 1, resting mainly on previously deposited tailings. This process is repeated as often as necessary. Note that each dyke requires roughly the same amount of earth and rock fill as the dam grows higher. There are 3 "raises" above the starter dyke in Figure 6.1, but there can be as many as 10 or more.

A downstream dam must start further upstream to allow for downstream expansion. Other than that, its starter dyke will be similar to the starter in an upstream dam. However, subsequent dykes require rapidly increasing amounts of fill, as is evident in Figure 6.1.

Downstream dams are more expensive than upstream because of the extra fill and land area required. But they are fundamentally more robust and less likely to fail catastrophically.[3] Upstream dams in contrast are more precarious, usually reliant on the underlying tailings to develop some degree of rigidity as they are compacted. Such dams must be monitored far more carefully throughout their life cycle to ensure that they are not at risk of catastrophic failure. Upstream dams are considered inappropriate in regions subject to flooding or earthquakes and are therefore banned in some parts of the world.

To summarise, downstream dams are inherently safer than upstream dams, but are more expensive to construct.[4]

Centreline dams are a compromise between the other 2 types. Each new dyke sits on top of the previous one and is supported by a long slope made of earth or rock

---

[1] Earthworks and Mining Watch Canada, *Safety First: Guidelines for Responsible Mine Tailings Management*, June 2020, p 6.

[2] Or as a ring dyke enclosure on flat land.

[3] International Commission on Large Dams (ICOLD) and United Nations Environment Programme (UNEP), Tailings dams risk of dangerous occurrences – Lessons learnt from practical experiences, *ICOLD Bulletin 121*, 2001. This authoritative report concluded that "dams built by the downstream .... method are much safer than those built by the upstream method" (p 24).

Likewise, a recent survey that found that "The normalised prevalence of past stability issues reported by active upstream facilities is twice that of downstream facilities...". Franks, D, Stringer, M, Baker, E, Valenta, R, et al, Lessons from Tailings Facility Data Disclosures, *GTR Compendium*, Chapter VII, p 85.

[4] Historically, most new construction has used the upstream method, although in the most recent decade, downstream construction is now the most common method for new construction. See Franks, D, Stringer, M, Baker, E, Valenta, R et al, op cit, p 91, Figure 4.

fill. The upstream end of each dyke sits on tailings. The total amount of fill in this method of construction is obviously less than for downstream construction.

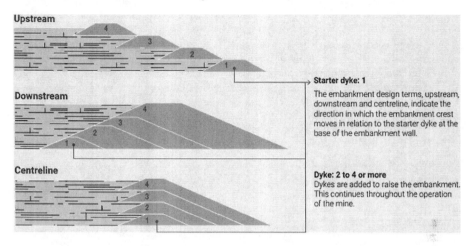

Figure 6.1: Common methods of tailings embankment construction[5]

Consider now what various geotechnical experts have had to say about upstream construction. In March 2018, a tailings facility in the state of New South Wales in Australia failed. The facility was part of the Cadia gold mine, owned by Newcrest, one of the world's largest gold mining companies. The failure occurred just 6 months after Newcrest was admitted as a full member of the ICMM. No injuries or fatalities were recorded. After the incident, Newcrest appointed a team of 4 independent experts to investigate. The investigation team was chaired by Nobert Morgenstern, one of the world's foremost geotechnical engineers, and included Dirk Van Zyl, a fellow member of our expert panel.

The construction of the Cadia dam began with downstream and centreline raises, with the last 7 raises all of upstream construction.[6] The report by the independent experts expressed reservations about the upstream method used at Cadia. The executive summary notes that Newcrest intended to continue operating the Cadia facility by upstream construction, after the failure, and it cautioned as follows:

> "It must be recognised that this implies management of loose, saturated, and potentially liquifiable tailings for the full life cycle of the facility. To avoid the type of failure that has been experienced in the Event, NML [Newcrest] should: ...".

The report then listed a number of actions including that Newcrest should install appropriate instrumentation to demonstrate that the foundation was behaving as intended.

[5] Baker et al, Mine Tailings Facilities: Overview and Industry Trends, in *GTR Compendium*, Chapter II, p 15.
[6] Jefferies, M, Morgenstern, NR, Van Zyl, D and Wates, J, *Report on NTSF Embankment Failure Cadia Valley Operations for Ashurst Australia*, 17 April 2019, p 7. newcrest.com/sites/default/files/2019-10/190417_Report%20on%20NTSF%20Embankment%20Failure%20at%20Cadia%20for%20Ashurst.pdf.

Elsewhere the report states:

> "It [Newcrest] should recognise that members of [the investigation team] take a more precautionary view with respect to upstream construction than has prevailed on site in the past ... [The passage continues, quoting Morgenstern] 'there is nothing wrong with upstream tailings dams provided that key principles are adhered to in the design, construction, and operation of such dams. Some 12 principles are outlined that should be recognised when upstream dams are proposed...it is essential to continually demonstrate by monitoring that the assumed unsaturated conditions in the buttress persist if relied upon in the design and that the buttress is behaving as intended'."

Taken together, these statements indicate that the support of these experts for upstream construction is heavily qualified.

Morgenstern's reference to "some 12 principles" draws on earlier work,[7] whose authors put the point more strongly as follows (they speak of 10 rather than 12 principles/rules):

> "Of the 10 rules, a 'score' of 9/10 will not necessarily have a better outcome than 2/10, *as any omission* creates immediate candidacy for an upstream tailings dam to join the list of facilities that have failed due to ignoring some or all of the rules". (Emphasis added.)[8]

This is a slightly obscure statement that may need to be read twice to reveal its full meaning. We can only agree with Earthworks and Mining Watch Canada on this matter when they say:

> "There is a broad consensus within the engineering community that engineering structures should be robust, with multiple back-ups and defence mechanisms. The need to obey ten rules with no margin for error does not constitute a safe basis for design".[9]

So what does Morgenstern have to say about countries such as Chile that have banned upstream construction? Is he critical of such bans? No. Here is what he says:

> "The Chilean regulation, as with most national/regional regulation, reflects more than design principles. It must reflect the maturity of the design community, procurement policies, quality assurance, land tenure, the degree of seismicity, and many other aspects of practice. Only the Chileans have the capacity to make these integrated judgments with respect to public safety in their own country".[10]

Morgenstern is here implicitly acknowledging that companies and the geotechnical engineers they employ may not have the necessary expertise or perhaps even the willingness to comply with his 12 principles, and that the state should act accordingly – in the interests of public safety.

Evans and Davies make a vital additional point in their chapter for the *GTR Compendium*.[11]

---

[7] Martin, TE and McRoberts, EC, Some consideration in the stability analysis of upstream tailings dams, *Proc. Tailings and Mine Waste '99*, Fort Collins, 1999, pp 287–302. researchgate.net/profile/ Ed_Mcroberts/publication/255509946_Some_considerations_in_the_stability_analysis_of_upstream_ tailings_dams/links/5865631408ae329d62045921/Some-considerations-in-the-stability-analysis-of- upstream-tailings-dams.pdf.
[8] Martin, TE, McRoberts, EC and Davies, MP, *A Tale of Four Upstream Tailings Dams*, (n.d.) citeseerx. ist.psu.edu/viewdoc/download?doi=10.1.1.532.7955&rep=rep1&type=pdf.
[9] Earthworks and Mining Watch Canada, op cit, p 12.
[10] Morgenstern, N, op cit, p 119.
[11] Evans, R and Davies, M, Creating and Retaining Knowledge and Expertise, *GTR Compendium*, Chapter XI, p 150.

> "... the main challenge [facing the mining industry] is one of ensuring that all those involved in the design, construction, management, monitoring, review and regulation of individual facilities possess the requisite knowledge and expertise to make informed decisions across the full operations lifecycle from design to decommissioning.
>
> Our assessment is that there is currently a relatively small group of specialists working in industry, consultancies, regulatory teams and as independent reviewers who possess deep technical capability in this area. Thereafter, there is a rapid fall-off of knowledge and expertise amongst operational management and other key actors such as regulators."

Given this widespread lack of expertise, even among regulators, the precautionary approach would be for governments to ban upstream construction, at least until the industry has the capacity to guarantee the safety of this method. Otherwise, we face the situation where dangerous facilities are being run potentially by inexpert people.

The member companies of the ICMM were opposed to any prohibition on upstream construction. On the other hand, NGOs representing the interests of project-affected people argue for total prohibition. Some even demand that the industry close all existing upstream facilities.

Moreover, it is noteworthy that one of the co-conveners, the PRI, was not opposed to the idea of prohibition in some circumstances. In its public submission it wrote:

> "[there is a] possibility that some types of dam are too risky in certain circumstances. **If the review considers this to be the case, ... this ought to be articulated. E.g. Upstream dams...**" (emphasis in original).

Likewise, outside of the constraints of the co-convened process, UNEP has argued the industry should "adopt a presumption against ... the use of upstream ... dams unless justified by independent review."[12]

It could be argued that Morgenstern's 12 principles are implicitly covered by the Standard in its current form and there is, therefore, no need to ban upstream dams in the Standard. But full compliance with the Standard can never be guaranteed, even for a facility that has been externally certified as compliant. Moreover, if a certified facility is sold there is no guarantee that the new owner will commit to the Standard. Given that full compliance is so critical in this case, we believe the precautionary principle should still apply.

We conclude that if the original documentation had not declared that a prohibition on upstream dams was out of scope, there might have been vigorous debate on this issue, leading possibly to some qualified form of prohibition in the final Standard.

---

[12] Roche, C, Thygesen, K and Baker, B, (Eds), *Mine Tailings Storage: Safety Is No Accident,* A UNEP Rapid Response Assessment, United Nations Environment Programme and GRID-Arendal, Nairobi and Arendal 2017, p 64. gridarendal-website-live.s3.amazonaws.com/production/documents/:s_document/371/original/RRA_MineTailings_lores.pdf?1510660693.

A ban on riverine disposal?

Another criticism levelled at the Standard is that it fails to ban riverine tailings disposal. Riverine disposal involves discarding tailings into the river system near a mine. This method tends to be used where the geotechnical, seismic and flood risks are so great that the mining company decides that an engineered facility is neither viable nor cost effective. It also occurs where the state is either unable or unwilling to prioritise people and the environment over tax and royalty windfalls. The 3 co-conveners agreed that the Standard would not cover or ban riverine tailings disposal.

At one level, the exclusion of riverine tailings from the Standard makes sense. The Standard aims to prevent the catastrophic failure of tailings *facilities*. If tailings are dumped in a river, then there is no storage mechanism. This method is literally not certifiable because there is no facility to certify. However, from our vantage point, if an operator fails to build a facility and instead deposits tailings into a river system, we would say that a flow failure has occurred. By excluding riverine disposal from the Standard, the co-conveners appear to be endorsing the practice.

The position of the co-conveners is curious, given the limited extent to which ICMM member companies use riverine tailings disposal. In what follows, we draw attention to 3 large-scale mines that use this method. ICMM members have a major stake in 2 of these, Porgera and Grasberg. We defer discussion on the third for a moment. Porgera and Grasberg have operated for decades using riverine disposal. In both cases, the practice is approved by the host states of Papua New Guinea and Indonesia.

The Porgera mine, which commenced operations in 1989, is located in a high mountainous area of Papua New Guinea. The mine is operated by the Porgera Joint Venture (PJV), in which Barrick Gold has a 47.5% share. Chinese company Zijin owns 47.5% with 5% held at the provincial level. The Porgera mine has one pit and several sprawling waste dumps. Two of the dumps are "stable" and 2 are "erodible". The 2 erodible dumps are designed that way — to erode straight into the river system.

The Grasberg mine, which commenced operations in 1987, is located in the highlands of West Papua. It is operated by PT Freeport Indonesia. Freeport-McMoRan owns a 48.8% share, with the majority share held by Inalum, Indonesia's state-owned mining company. PT Freeport Indonesia describes its approach to tailings management as "controlled riverine tailings disposal" on the basis that it is approved by the Government of Indonesia.

The effects of riverine tailings disposal from these 2 operations are well documented and include, most obviously, overbank flooding from increased sedimentation and vegetation die-back along the riverbank. These impacts have devastated foraging and hunting grounds. Fish stocks have been depleted, significantly reducing the protein intake of local people, and there are longstanding reports of skin diseases and other chronic health effects.

PT Freeport Indonesia claims on its website that:

> "The river is not used for potable water, agriculture, fishing or other domestic or commercial uses, nor was it used for these purposes before operations began".

However, years of work by researchers, international NGOs and advocates for local people suggest that this statement is wrong.

It is noteworthy that on its website, PT Freeport Indonesia justifies the use of riverine disposal as follows:

"If any conventional tailings system had been selected and implemented, it likely would have structurally failed by now".[13]

It might have drawn a radically different conclusion, namely, if riverine disposal is the only available method of tailings disposal, then mining should not go ahead. That is the position that BHP came to with respect to its Ok Tedi mine, as we shall see in a moment.

The fact that the Standard does not cover riverine disposal avoids placing the practices of these companies in the spotlight. Barrick Gold and Freeport-McMoRan are ICMM members that were active in negotiations about the Standard. Both sent representatives to interact directly with the expert panel to deliver the ICMM's feedback. In fact, the CEO of Freeport-McMoRan travelled to South Africa to meet with the expert panel in person.[14] It is clear that these 2 companies would have vetoed any attempt by the expert panel to expand the scope of the Standard to cover riverine disposal.

The third major large-scale mine to use riverine tailings disposal is Ok Tedi, which began operating in Papua New Guinea in the mid-1980s. The mine is now operated by Ok Tedi Mining Limited (OTML), which is wholly owned by the Government of Papua New Guinea. Previously, OTML was jointly owned by BHP (52%) and lesser-known Canadian company Inmet (18%), with the remainder held by the government. BHP and Inmet no longer have a shareholding in the operation.[15]

While the history of Ok Tedi is deeply complex and highly controversial, our focus is limited to one aspect of this operation — tailings. The original design for the Ok Tedi mine included an engineered tailings facility. In the early construction period, the foundations of what was to be the storage facility were inundated by a landslide and destroyed. Eager for the mine to commence operations, the government approved the construction of an interim facility so that operations could commence while the project investigated storage alternatives. But an alternative was not found. When the capacity of the interim facility was reached within a couple of years, the government approved the disposal of treated tailings into the river system as a permanent method of waste disposal. Later, waste rock was added as the operation's waste rock dumps were also destroyed by landslides. It did not take long for the tailings and other waste streams to clog the river system with sediment and devastate an entire river system.

When the scale of the devastation came to light in the late 1980s, conservation and human rights organisations launched an intense campaign against BHP. Over a period of 10 years, BHP was shamed, sued and vilified for its involvement in the project. It eventually bowed to pressure and explored the possibility of closing the project early. Despite its majority shareholding, BHP could not act unilaterally. Neither Inmet nor the Government of Papua New Guinea agreed to close the mine. With its lesser global profile and its smaller share, Inmet

---

[13] Freeport McMoRan, fcx.com/sustainability/environment/tailings/controlled-riverine-tailings-management.
[14] Other companies to send representatives to interface with the expert panel as part of the ICMM's engagement in the process were Antofagasta Minerals, Teck and BHP. Rio Tinto and Anglo American also attended a meeting of the Advisory Group as observers.
[15] Declaration of interest. One of us (Kemp) was employed by BHP from 1996 to 2003.

was not subject to public pressure. The Papua New Guinea Government took the view that the benefits of the mine far outweighed the costs. Agreements struck with villagers downstream from the operation included compensation and development benefits to offset the mine's impacts and, as dredging began, to minimise some of the consequences. Local opposition dimmed. BHP was left to orchestrate its own withdrawal strategy.

To avoid being seen to profit from the sale of their share of the operation, BHP divested its share to a sustainable development trust fund for the people of Papua New Guinea and the Western Province, in perpetuity.[16]

At the time that BHP announced its withdrawal in 2001, the then CEO (Paul Anderson) admitted that Ok Tedi was "not compatible" with the company's values and that BHP should "never have become involved" in a project with this kind of negative environmental and social footprint. He pledged that from that point forward, BHP would not consider investing in any new projects that use riverine tailings disposal. Since this time, BHP has maintained a policy of no riverine tailings disposal.

Meanwhile, Ok Tedi continues to mine. The company's website says:

> "The riverine discharge of tailings and waste rock management continues to be the most significant long-term environmental challenge for OTML. This has had adverse environmental impacts on the Ok Tedi and Fly River systems and associated eco-systems, which in turn has impacted the livelihood and cultural life of the communities who live along the river corridor."

And yet, despite this history, BHP did not speak out on the issue of riverine tailings during the GTR process, not even to clarify its own position. Curiously, none of the papers in the *GTR compendium* addresses the issue in any substantive way.

There are various factors that may have contributed to the ICMM's refusal from the outset to contemplate a ban on riverine disposal in the Standard. One would have been to avoid antagonising member companies using the method, such as Barrick and Freeport. Another would have been the view that riverine disposal cannot give rise to an acute catastrophic failure, although we would argue that it can have long-term catastrophic consequences for local people. The issue of acute versus chronic failure is discussed later in this chapter.

ICMM members might also have been concerned that banning riverine tailings disposal was a "slippery slope", opening the way for bans on upstream facilities, deep sea tailings placement and the like. These technologies are more widely used by ICMM member companies across the board.

Finally, we note here that the United Nations rapid assessment report immediately after the Samarco disaster made a series of recommendations. As the lead agency on this assessment, UNEP proposed the establishment of a stakeholder forum to facilitate international strengthening of tailings dam regulation and 3 priority actions. The second of these actions, "failure prevention", includes a series of sub-points, including "ban or commit to not use riverine tailings disposal". Further,

---

[16] This strategy later disintegrated as the trust was taken over by the state, but by this time BHP had distanced itself from the project.

the report suggests that this include "a presumption against the use of submarine tailings disposal [...] unless justified by independent review".[17]

In its role as co-convener of the Standard, UNEP could have argued for a ban on riverine tailings disposal, or more clearly articulated its own position at key moments during the GTR process to better profile this issue. This would have been consistent with its earlier statements. Yet UNEP seems to have acquiesced on this particular issue, apparently in the interests of achieving consensus among the co-conveners on the broader Standard.

If the GTR was an exercise in lifting the performance bar on tailings management and addressing the issue of the industry's low credibility in the eyes of its stakeholders, then engaging on the issue of riverine tailings disposal could have been an "easy win". The fact that this "win" was not pursued is a reflection of the political process in which the co-conveners were engaged.

Chronic impacts of chronic failure

Some issues were out of scope from the outset, like upstream facilities and riverine tailings disposal. Other issues were negotiated over the course of the GTR process. The definition of "catastrophic failure" and the treatment of "chronic impacts" were addressed in this way. In this section, we begin by explaining a few key terms in order to examine how the industry sought to contain the scope of the Standard on these issues.

For tailings engineers, the term "catastrophic failure" points to the failure of a facility. For environmental and social scientists, the term also indicates the scale and magnitude of impacts – a catastrophe. There was a significant period of time where the definition of catastrophic failure was not clear. Each time the ICMM insisted that the expert panel focus on "catastrophic failure", some of us would focus on the facility and others on the impact. After many discussions, this tension was resolved and a definition was agreed that encompassed both facility failure and the impact on people and the environment. The final version of the Standard includes the following definition:

> "A tailings facility failure that results in material disruption to social, environmental and local economic systems. Such failures are a function of the interaction between hazard exposure, vulnerability, and the capacity of people and systems to respond. Catastrophic events typically involve numerous adverse impacts, at different scales and over different timeframes, including loss of life, damage to physical infrastructure or natural assets, and disruption to lives, livelihoods, and social order. Operators may be affected by damage to assets, disruption to operations, financial loss, or negative impact to reputation. Catastrophic failures exceed the capacity of affected people to cope using their own resources, triggering the need for outside assistance in emergency response, restoration and recovery efforts".

Having resolved that a "catastrophic failure" includes the facility failure and the consequences of that failure, the question became: what kind of failure and what kind of impact?

---

[17] This UNEP/Grid-Arendal recommendation also includes the presumption against the use of covers on tailings dams and the use of upstream and cascading tailings dams, addressed in the preceding section of this chapter.

On the question of failures, these can be acute or chronic. Acute failure constitutes a rapid and sudden shock. Mount Polley, Samarco and Brumadinho were acute catastrophic events with clearly observable impacts. These failures happened suddenly, without warning (putting aside the fact that these failures could have been foreseen). The public outrage after these events is, in part, due to closeness in time between the moment of facility failure and the moment of impact on people. The Brumadinho disaster was filmed and the shock of seeing this event unfold before one's eyes propelled public demand for urgent and radical industry change.

By contrast, a chronic failure occurs over time, almost in slow motion and may not be easily observable. Chronic failures can also be cumulative in nature, involving issues that "add up" to a failure of significant scale and magnitude – prolonged seepage, undetected instability and fugitive dust from a dry stack. In other words, failures can happen quickly – in a split second – or over time. Either way, they can have immediate and long-term impacts on people and the environment.

The industry insisted that the Standard focus on the sudden failure of tailings facilities, and accepted that this brought into play both immediate and long-term impacts. This is one reason why "long-term recovery" appears in the standard, in recognition that sudden catastrophic failures will have long-term, chronic impacts that need to be addressed.

During the public consultation, however, the expert panel learned that many stakeholders had a broader conception of catastrophic failure, and expected the Standard to include chronic impacts from *chronic failure*. In fact, for some people, chronic failure at existing facilities was a far more pressing concern than an acute failure. Some stakeholders contended that if chronic failure at existing facilities were overlooked, then the Standard would be ignoring the more common impacts that many communities suffer day-to-day.

When he visited South Africa during the public consultation round, the panel chair was confronted with a particularly insidious example of chronic failure – where communities alleged that they were being exposed, over a period of years, to radioactive dust from the tailings of abandoned uranium mines. Members of the community explained that the government had forcibly moved them onto land containing the tailings. They complained of cancers, skin rashes and chronic breathing issues, and said that the government had provided respirators but had done nothing more, despite the fact that the original owners had lodged financial bonds with the government to cover remediation of the site. Community advocates had commissioned their own epidemiology studies to help draw attention to the issues. At the public consultation, advocates showed the panel chair photos of the site and the community, and implored him not to overlook chronic impacts at existing facilities.

After hearing about this case and other similar cases from the public consultation, the panel contemplated requiring operators to address the chronic impacts of chronic failure (recognising that the impact would still have to be of a scale and magnitude that was considered to be catastrophic).

The ICMM considered the inclusion of chronic impacts of a chronic failure to be "significant expansion of scope". In its feedback to the panel, it explained that this would make the Standard unwieldy and costly, and would drastically reduce the likelihood that companies would ever endorse it. The ICMM's concern was obvious – this could require the upgrade of older facilities, which in some cases could be a very costly exercise.

In the end, and for practical reasons, chronic failure is not mentioned in the Standard. Chronic impacts are mentioned, but only for new facilities. Requirement 3.3 says:

> "For new tailings facilities ... assess the social, environmental and local economic impacts of the tailings facility and its potential failure throughout its lifecycle. Where impact assessments predict material acute or chronic impacts, the Operator shall develop, document and implement impact mitigation and management plans using the mitigation hierarchy."

Existing facilities are not required to assess or address chronic impacts of chronic failures. This means that silent and slow-motion failures at existing facilities require no action on the part of operators as part of implementing the Standard. As long as operators prevent acute failure of existing facilities and commit to dealing with chronic impacts and long-term recovery in the aftermath of an acute failure, they are in conformity with the Standard. The industry successfully restricted the scope of the Standard on this issue.

Financial *assurance* and *insurance*

When mines reach the end of their life, tailings dams and dumps must be closed so that they are safe in perpetuity. This means not only that the risk of acute catastrophic failure is negligible, but also that there is no long-term threat to the health of local people or to the environment from substances leaking into the atmosphere or nearby bodies of water. We described this problem in the previous section.

Historically, some companies have either chosen to ignore the problem and leave local residents to their fate, or they have gone bankrupt and been unable to meet the considerable expense of closing the facility so that it is safe in perpetuity.

The expert panel responded to this problem by proposing companies should provide *assurance* that they had the financial capacity to close facilities safely, no matter what their circumstances at the time of closure. This would take the form of a financial instrument, such as a bond deposited with a third party that would be available to meet the company's closure obligations, if needed. Self-bonding would also be possible if the operator could demonstrate it had sufficient tangible assets to cover such costs.

A second financial issue is *insurance* against acute catastrophic tailings facility failure at any stage in the life cycle of the facility. The liability costs of such failures can be billions of dollars, which smaller companies may be unable to pay. The panel proposed that companies should have liability insurance to cover such costs. Self-insurance would be possible where the company could demonstrate that it had sufficient tangible assets.

The ICMM objected strongly to both these proposed requirements. In each case, the primary reason was that the requirement "goes well beyond the *contemplated* scope of the review" (emphasis added).

Recall here that the scope of the review was not tightly specified in the foundation document and was "not limited" to matters initially specified. Accordingly, it cannot be said that the expert panel had gone beyond that scope. What happened was that the panel had gone beyond the scope *contemplated by the ICMM CEOs*. It should be noted, too, that UNEP strongly supported the proposed requirements, while the PRI was generally supportive, but preferred to stay at the level of principle rather than detail.

Unfortunately, these 2 provisions were largely vetoed by the CEOs in the red-lining that occurred before the consultation draft of the Standard was released for public comment (see Chapter 4). They were replaced with far more anodyne statements. This meant that people who responded to the call for comments did not have a chance to react to the thinking of the expert panel on this matter. There was, however, enough feedback to prompt the re-introduction of these ideas in the version that went finally to the co-conveners for their consideration.

At this final stage, the views of the ICMM again prevailed. In relation to assurance bonds, the CEOs argued that smaller companies might not be able to afford them, which would inhibit adoption of the Standard. For larger companies it would affect their cash position unnecessarily. There was little point in trying to meet these objections because the ICMM was irrevocably opposed to the inclusion of any requirement for financial instruments in the Standard. Accordingly, the requirement that companies post a bond or be allowed to self-bond if they can demonstrate "sufficient tangible assets" was replaced with the requirement that they "confirm that *adequate financial capacity* is available".

The ICMM uses the phrase "adequate financial capacity", while the panel required "sufficient tangible assets". What is the difference? One possibility is that a company might plan to fund closure from the mine's *future income stream*, and that evidence of expected future income might be treated as evidence of *adequate financial capacity*. If so, this is a much more uncertain form of assurance than the panel was requiring. This is just one way in which "adequate financial capacity" can fall short of "sufficient tangible assets".

We note here that the ICMM was supported in its view by a submission from the International Finance Corporation (IFC), also represented on the GTR advisory group. The IFC describes itself as "a sister organization of the World Bank ... and the largest global development institution focused on the private sector in developing countries. [Its goals are to] end extreme poverty and promote shared prosperity in every country".[18] The IFC guidelines state that:

> "The costs associated with mine closure and post-closure activities, including post-closure care, should be included in business feasibility analyses during the planning and design stages. Minimum considerations should include the availability of all necessary funds, by appropriate financial instruments, to cover the cost of closure ... Funding should be by either a cash accrual system or a financial guarantee."[19]

---

[18] IFC, About IFC.ifc.org/wps/wcm/connect/corp_ext_content/ifc_external_corporate_site/about+ifc_new.
[19] IFC, Environmental, Health and Safety Guidelines for Mining, 10 December 2007, p 24. ifc. org/wps/wcm/connect/595149ed-8bef-4241-8d7c-50e91d8e459d/Final%2B-%2BMining. pdf?MOD=AJPERES&CVID=jqezAit&tid=1323153264157.

In spite of this, the IFC was concerned the expert panel's proposal might jeopardise "the ability to deliver ... [their] international investment options into IDA[20] or FCS[21] countries". It further observed that "some members of the panel were indifferent to the impact on the smaller or less competitive part of the industry". This discrepancy between the IFC guidelines and its *de facto* investment practices was never explained to the panel.

As for the other financial requirement, liability insurance, this proposal was simply eliminated. In its comments on the consultation draft, the ICMM expressed the view that insurance was not related to the prevention of catastrophic failure and was, therefore, by implication, out of scope.[22] A few words about *insurance* were introduced in the final *assurance* requirement, but they were largely meaningless. This was part of a compromise struck between the co-conveners to reach agreement on this issue. For the PRI, however, the matter is not over. It plans to pursue the issue of insurance outside the framework of the Standard.

The debate over these issues among the co-conveners was intense and prolonged. The ICMM gave no ground, UNEP gave a great deal, and the PRI adopted a mediator role between the ICMM and UNEP. In the end, the only way an agreement was going to be reached was if UNEP and the PRI capitulated to the ICMM.

Accountability and governance

The initial GTR documentation listed a series of questions for possible consideration, including the following:

1. "What are the cultural, behavioural and incentive barriers within companies that block better management of tailings facilities?"

This is a clear invitation to consider bonus arrangements and their impact on tailings facility safety.

2. "How can company tailings experts be more empowered through internal governance structures ... ?"

One of the most important internal governance structures is the structure of reporting lines – who reports to whom. This question was therefore an invitation for the panel to consider reporting arrangements and to propose alternatives.

3. "What changes should be considered to enable significant risks relating to tailings storage facilities to be elevated to senior management, e.g. Executive Committee level?"

These 3 questions all relate to governance. Questions of governance were therefore explicitly within scope.

We surmise that these questions represent input from UNEP and the PRI since they drew attention to them at various stages in the process. We also surmise that

[20] International Development Association.
[21] Fragile and conflict-affected situations.
[22] ICMM submission in response to the Global Tailings Standard consultation draft of November 2019 against Topic/Principle/Requirement 2.6, p 6. globaltailingsreview.org/wp-content/uploads/2020/07/International-Council-on-Mining-and-Metals-response.pdf.

ICMM members failed to understand their full significance at the time, since they subsequently argued that some of these matters were out of scope or inappropriate for inclusion in the Standard.

In relation to incentives, the ICMM said subsequently:

> "The Standard must refrain from setting requirements for remuneration, compensation or bonuses for various personnel."

And in relation to the panel's proposed reporting arrangements, the ICMM said they were "flawed, prescriptive and not appropriate for inclusion in a Standard".[23] In other words, these matters were beyond scope.

The panel gained the distinct impression that, apart from specific arguments about scope, many of the ICMM CEOs believed that it was their prerogative to decide how they structured their corporations and how they remunerated their staff, and that it was in principle unacceptable for the Standard to interfere with this prerogative. This was never articulated in writing, but it was conveyed to the panel in other ways.

In relation to the third question above, the ICMM was more accommodating. It accepted that decision-making about significant risks should be elevated to a senior manager, an accountable executive, as specified in several of the requirements in the Standard.

These matters are discussed further in Chapter 8.

Affected communities

One of the most contested questions about scope was whether or not the Standard should include any requirements about local communities. Of course, the purpose of the Standard was to ensure their safety, but other than that, the ICMM's initial view was that it was inappropriate to have requirements in the Standard spelling out the rights of project-affected people. This was beyond scope. The battle over this issue was fought over a prolonged period with various twists and turns. We say no more here because it is the subject of the next chapter.

Conclusion

A primary way in which the ICMM sought to protect its members' interests was by arguing that the requirements the panel were proposing went beyond the scope of the global tailings review. Certain matters were explicitly out of scope, as specified in the foundation document, which effectively tied the panel's hands. Others were not so clearly out of scope and were vigorously contested. In these matters the ICMM generally, but not always, got its way. Its strongest card in these cases was to argue that a proposal was unrealistic and would render mining uneconomic. While UNEP and the PRI were both in favour of broadening the scope, they were generally not in a position to resist the "realism" argument. In following chapters, we look at some of these contested issues in more detail.

---

[23] ibid, comment box p 39.

CHAPTER 7

Affected communities

This chapter describes how key social and community aspects of the Standard fared in the process of negotiation. It also explains how the final stages of the negotiations were influenced by a major incident that had nothing to do with tailings, but everything to do with how the industry engages with affected communities. This was the destruction of priceless cultural heritage in Western Australia by Rio Tinto. What we have since learned about this event helps to demonstrate why the panel insisted upon specific requirements in the Standard and why those requirements are so important in enabling affected communities to resist the power of the industry.

We begin this chapter by discussing the first of the Standard's 7 topics – Affected Communities – before honing in on 2 key concepts: "participation" and "free, prior and informed consent" (FPIC). We track the journey of these concepts through the construction of the Standard and explain where they landed. On some topics, the panel was successful in pushing for requirements it viewed as fundamental to the aims of the Standard. On others, it was not. At some points, readers may find it helpful to refer to the timeline of key dates in Appendix 2.

Prioritising the issue of affected communities

The preamble to the Standard explains that the requirements are not presented in a chronological order but follow a different logic. The positioning of the section on affected communities at the beginning of the Standard is a symbolic acknowledgement of the disastrous effects that tailings facility failures can have on local communities, and is intended to send a strong signal about what is most important – ensuring people are not harmed by tailings facility failures. The affected communities topic was not positioned in this way in the first drafts of the Standard. There was a prolonged period of negotiation before the final positioning was agreed.

Initially, the International Council for Mining and Metals (ICMM) was deeply troubled by the inclusion of social aspects in the Standard. Interestingly, though, its statement at the official launch in August 2020 gives no hint of the earlier concerns. It says that the Standard:

> "... sets a new, global benchmark to achieve strong social, environmental and technical outcomes in tailings management, with a strong emphasis on accountability and disclosure".[1]

The inference is that by the end of the process, ICMM member companies supported the inclusion of social aspects in the Standard, and the positioning of them at the beginning of the Standard. But this was not the case at the outset.

Some of our earliest engagements with the ICMM were through its working group tasked with developing technical guidance to support the Standard (see Chapter 4).

---

[1] ICMM, News: The Global Industry Standard on Tailings Management, 12 August 2020. icmm.com/en-gb/news/2020/gistm-new-global-benchmark.

This group comprised tailings facility engineers and other tailings and technical specialists. It did not include other disciplinary areas. The idea that the Standard would cover anything other than the very technical aspects of tailings facilities seemed to come as a surprise to this working group. This is despite the fact that the panel comprised a majority whose primary expertise lay outside the engineering domain (in sociology, human rights, environment and law) and who were of course going to emphasise issues relevant to their own disciplinary domains.

A number of teleconferences were held between the panel and the working group in the initial phase of the work. On these calls, the panel was asked to explain the topics that would be covered in the Standard (and likewise the working group explained the content of its planned guidance document). The working group suggested that the social aspects be removed from the "auditable" component of the Standard. It argued that those aspects were unnecessary for 2 reasons. First, member companies already had standards that covered social performance, and second, including them would detract from the technical aspects. The panel disagreed. It chose not to relegate the social and community aspects of the Standard to the background and proceeded to the public consultation with these aspects treated as both central and deeply connected to the technical aspects (although at this stage they were not positioned as the first topic in the Standard, see below).

In its public response to the consultation draft of November 2019, the ICMM reiterated the view of the working group on behalf of all its members:

> "We strongly believe that the original objective of developing an international Standard for the safe and secure management of mine tailings facilities to prevent catastrophic failures should remain central to the purpose and content of the Global Tailings Standard [...] In our view the draft document for consultation contains many requirements which are either only indirectly related to this objective, or do not influence the stability, safety and management of tailings facilities. This is especially the case for broad-based requirements involving environmental, human rights, and social aspects."[2]

The expert panel worked under constant threat that the Standard would be rejected by industry with ICMM members collectively wielding veto rights. While this gave companies a strong bargaining chip, it was not strong enough to persuade the panel to demote or remove the social and community aspects of the Standard.

The public consultation process brought to light a broad range of views on the Standard. Some submissions aligned with ICMM views. For instance, the Minerals Council South Africa said:

> "Advocating zero tolerance [to human fatality] in respect of tailings failure may dilute the technical (standards) focus of the Standard ..."[3]

Likewise, a public submission from a consulting geotechnical engineer who served on the advisory group said:

---

[2] Email responses to the Global Tailings Standard consultation draft of November 2019, ICMM, p 1. globaltailingsreview.org/consultation-report/email-responses/.
[3] Email responses, op cit, Minerals Council South Africa, p 3.

"The overemphasis on governance and social does not proportionally reflect the root problem of safe design, which is largely technical [...] Social aspects are very important, however discretion is required with overemphasizing the social aspects related to dam failure as the reality is that most dams do not fail ..."[4]

Other submissions were supportive of including social aspects. In fact, some groups argued that the social aspects did not go far enough. The Human Rights Law Centre, for one, said that the Standard should be strengthened in this regard:

"[It needs] to better acknowledge the value of, and incorporate, community knowledge into an operation's knowledge base, and promote the co-creation of knowledge between communities and operators. Doing so will help reassure at-risk communities and then to enable them to engage on more equal terms with operators on tailings facilities risks."[5]

The public consultation draft presented "affected communities" as the second topic, after "knowledge base". In the final version, "affected communities" is first. The decision to swap these topics came quite late in the process, just before the panel presented the final draft to the co-conveners for their endorsement in March 2020. The chair asked the panel to consider putting "affected communities" first – a move that some panel members had earlier suggested, but had not been fully accepted within the group. By the time the chair made his proposal, the panel as a whole was ready to take this stand, and the "affected communities" topic moved to first place, where it stayed for the remainder of the process.

While we are pleased with the position and prominence of the affected communities' requirements, other outcomes were not so pleasing. One of these is the absence of the word "participation".

Participation in decisions

In November 2019, the panel had finalised its draft Standard for the public consultation process. It provided the draft to the co-conveners, not for approval, but as a courtesy, prior to the public consultation. Requirement 3.2[6] of this courtesy draft read as follows:

"Meaningfully engage project-affected people throughout the tailings facility lifecycle *in a manner that enables their participation in decisions that affect them, including decisions that affect their risk exposure level.*" (Italics added for following comparison.)

This requirement was unacceptable to the ICMM CEOs, who "red-lined" it, as described in Chapter 4, just days before the draft was scheduled for release to the public. The United Nations Environment Program (UNEP) and the Principles for Responsible Investment (PRI) had both expected the panel's draft to go to public consultation unaltered. But the ICMM group of CEOs exercised their veto power at this pivotal moment, demanding that changes be made.

---

[4] Email responses, op cit, Harvey McLeod, p 1.
[5] Email responses, op cit, Human Rights Law Centre, p 6.
[6] Note that this numbering refers to the consultation draft, not the final draft. The consultation draft, of November 2019, is available on the GTR website – globaltailingsreview.org.

The altered wording was as follows:

> "Meaningfully engage project-affected people throughout the tailings facility lifecycle *regarding the matters that affect them.*" (Italics added for comparison.)

As can be seen by comparing the 2 versions, the second is very much weaker than the first. Specifically, the CEOs deleted 3 key ideas from the requirement: *participation, decisions* and *risk exposure.* It is clear that they did not accept that project-affected people should participate in decisions about the risk that a tailings facility poses to them or their families.

The panel had good reason for including these ideas. People's right to know and to decide on their exposure to industrial hazards and their associated risks is a well-established principle in international law and mainstream development policy. It is also a reason for requiring public access to information in the latter parts of the Standard. The Standard was intended to enable project-affected people to have an active role in determining whether, and if so, how, they would tolerate the imposition of risk by a mining company. As things stood, many communities were exposed to industrial risk without their prior knowledge.

To keep the process moving, the chair conceded to the demands of the CEOs, having confidence that the public consultation would require that some of the original intent and wording be restored. The other co-conveners accepted these alterations and the advisory group was also informed.

The expert panel was outraged at this procedural breach, but the chair counselled patience and trust in the process. Neither the panel, nor the advisory group, broke ranks on this, largely out of respect for the chair and an implicit acceptance that the process needed to run its course. Nonetheless, the panel was left to defend a consultation draft that had been weakened and now contained technical inaccuracies. This placed the panel in an awkward position during the public consultation process.

Over time, with feedback from the public and the advisory group, support from the chair and input from the other 2 co-conveners, the panel did regain some ground. The public consultation process, in particular, provided strong reason to reinstate some of the original wording. For instance, a submission from a major labour union that covers mine workers, among others, said:

> "The only people with the moral authority to assess a risk, are those who face the risk. Any risk assessment done without the full participation of those who face the risk (workers, members of potentially affected communities, etc.) is illegitimate."[7]

Likewise, in its public response to the draft Standard, the PRI said:

> "Some of those who promote the rights of project-affected people emphasise the importance of their involvement and participation in decisions that affect them. This is absent from the requirements, and all community involvement is couched in the technical terminology of 'meaningful engagement'."[8]

---

[7]   Email responses, op cit, Brian Kohler of IndustriALL, p 2.
[8]   Email responses, op cit, Principles for Responsible Investment, p 3.

The PRI is one of the co-conveners, and this submission demonstrates the gulf that existed between the ICMM and the PRI on this point. The CEO red-lining was an opportunistic exercise of power designed to pre-empt debate on this issue. However, it ultimately served to strengthen the resolve of the expert panel and the chair to resist the propensity of the ICMM member companies to insert themselves into what was meant to be an independent process.

Following the consultation, the expert panel managed to reinstate the word *decisions* into the text by limiting it to *decisions that may have a bearing on public safety and the integrity of the tailings facility*. This does not quite reflect the panel's original intent of ensuring that people have some power in decisions that affect them, including their level of risk exposure. Nonetheless, it was the best that could be achieved at the time. The panel also added wording to ensure that this decision-making process is supported by the provision of information to project-affected people.[9]

In the final version of this requirement, the relevant section reads as follows[10]:

> "Demonstrate that project-affected people are meaningfully engaged throughout the tailings facility lifecycle ... in decisions that may have a bearing on public safety and the integrity of the tailings facility. The Operator shall share information to support this process."

The word *participation* is missing and never made it back into any of the requirements concerning affected communities. The result is that companies retained their right to impose risk on local people, and avoided an explicit requirement compelling them to enable people's participation in project-related decisions.

Somewhat ironically, the industry did accept that affected people could participate in the clean-up after a catastrophic failure. The word *participation* appears briefly in the latter part of the Standard in the last topic "Emergency Response and Long-Term Recovery". In brief, the Standard specifies a right to participate in decisions *after* a failure, but not *before* the failure. This is unacceptable and it is something that hopefully can be changed in future iterations of the Standard.

We have not yet commented on the term "meaningful engagement", which is present in all versions of the requirement. This term is defined in the Standard's glossary, drawing on definitions used by major international and multilateral agencies and organisations, such as the United Nations (UN), the International Finance Corporation (IFC) and the Organisation for Economic Co-operation and Development (OECD). The definition explains that meaningful engagement involves a process whereby operators have an obligation to:

- consult and listen to stakeholder perspectives

- integrate those perspectives into business decisions

- implement measures to overcome structural and practical barriers to the participation of diverse groups of people

---

[9] For a discussion on the corporate prerogative to impose risk see: Owen, JR, and Kemp, D, Displaced by mine waste: the social consequences of industrial risk-taking, *Extractive Industries and Society* 2019, 6(2): pp 424–427.

[10] Requirement 1.3 in the final version of the Standard. The requirement is abbreviated here, so as to focus on the issue of relevance to this discussion.

- ■ enable access to material of information that stakeholders can reasonably understand

- ■ ensure accountability for engagement process and outcomes.

It will be noted that the third bullet point refers to "participation of diverse groups of people". This is a general reference to the participation of groups of people and does not specifically mention participation in decisions about risk exposure. In short, while the requirement does specify that companies must meaningfully engage with project-affected people, meaningful engagement is unlikely to be interpreted as requiring that project-affected people be able to participate in decisions about the risks to which they are exposed. We can only hope that some future independent entity will prove us wrong about this.

Throughout the process, and right up until the final weeks of the expert panel's work, there was discussion about what meaningful engagement *really* meant. Some panel members relayed doubts expressed to them by industry representatives about the auditability of the term. Moreover, many in the industry remain uncomfortable with the idea of shared decision-making – particularly with people who may not have the technical ability to understand complex information and who were not seen to be rational or scientific in their approach.

The contest over FPIC

Shortly after the panel delivered its draft to the co-conveners on 10 March 2020 for their final round of negotiations, COVID-19 intervened, delaying this process. In this section, we explain how this delay became consequential for the FPIC requirement – free, prior and informed consent. While there were several other contentious matters on the table for these negotiations, we focus on this requirement in particular. Before describing the controversy, we provide a short explanation of FPIC and why it is important.

First and foremost, FPIC is intended to serve a mechanism to safeguard, or protect, the rights of indigenous peoples, including their land and resource rights and their right to self-determination. These rights are protected under numerous instruments of international law.[11] In the context of mining, it means that developers cannot rely on approval from the state, before mining indigenous peoples' lands. They must also obtain consent from the traditional landowners. Such consent implies the capacity to either grant or withhold consent.

FPIC effectively enables indigenous peoples to determine – themselves – whether or not mining should proceed on their lands and, if so, under what conditions. These conditions usually include agreed processes for managing impacts, compensation for loss or damage, and benefits, such as royalties, employment and business development opportunities, and other community investments and contributions.

History shows, however, that indigenous peoples' rights are not always recognised or protected by states or respected by mining companies. FPIC is not always obtained, and

---

[11] Two key instruments are the International Labour Organization Convention (ILO) 169, ilo.org/dyn/normlex/en/f?p=NORMLEXPUB:12100:0::NO::P12100_ILO_CODE:C169, and the UN Declaration on the Rights of Indigenous Peoples (UNDRIP), un.org/development/desa/indigenouspeoples/declaration-on-the-rights-of-indigenous-peoples.html.

where attempts to obtain FPIC are made, the process is often inadequate. In 2013, the UN Special Rapporteur on the rights of indigenous peoples, James Anaya, observed that:

> "... the business model that still prevails in most places for the extraction of natural resources within indigenous territories is not one that is fully conducive to the fulfilment of indigenous peoples' rights, particularly their self-determination, proprietary and cultural rights in relation to the affected lands and resources."[12]

Over the past 10 years, in particular, and under great public pressure to address this issue, mining companies have begun to include FPIC in their corporate policy commitments. This has been contentious. We say contentious because even though the pre-requisites of "free", "prior" and "informed" seem straightforward, what constitutes FPIC in any given situation is often contested, as we shall see.

Further, there is often a misconception that indigenous peoples want to use FPIC to stop mining. While this may be the case in some circumstances, it is certainly not always the case. Many indigenous peoples are open to mining on their lands and territories, but first want to ensure that the things that are important to them, such as cultural heritage and sacred landscapes, are protected, *and* that they can benefit from mining. Industry fear that the "veto" will be used to block mining has driven the industry's objections to key concepts like "participation" and "consent".

With this brief background, we now return to the Standard. We are primarily concerned with tracing the process by which FPIC was introduced into the Standard. As a preliminary matter, we comment on the introduction of the concept of *human rights* in the Standard.

In the initial stages of the expert panel's work, the idea that respect for human rights might be included in the Standard was dismissed as "over-the-top", even by some within the panel. As the process developed, however, and with input from business and human rights experts and members of the advisory group, all members of the panel and the chair agreed that human rights warranted inclusion in the Standard. So it was that respect for human rights was included as a standalone requirement in the public consultation draft of November 2019.[13]

As for FPIC, it was mentioned only in the footnote relating to the requirement to respect human rights. The last sentence of the footnote read:

> "Demonstrating respect for indigenous people's rights may involve obtaining their 'free prior and informed consent' (FPIC), as outlined in the ICMM Indigenous Peoples and Mining Position Statement."

The public consultation generated many comments and submissions from indigenous and civil society groups affirming the importance of the human rights-related requirements in the Standard. Several groups noted, however, that FPIC appeared only in a footnote, and suggested that it be elevated to a requirement.[14] For instance, in their written submission, the Northern Confluence Initiative said:

---

[12] Anaya, J, *Report of the Special Rapporteur on the rights of indigenous peoples*, Human Rights Council 1 July 2013, United Nations. ohchr.org/EN/HRBodies/HRC/RegularSessions/Session24/Documents/A-HRC-24-41_en.pdf.

[13] For further reading, see: United Nations Human Rights, *Guiding Principles on Business and Human Rights*, 2011. ohchr.org/documents/publications/guidingprinciplesbusinesshr_en.pdf.

[14] Email responses, op cit, Northern Confluence Initiative, p 1.

> "There should be an explicit requirement for the Free, Prior and Informed Consent (FPIC) of Indigenous Peoples in order for a mine to even be developed."

Likewise, Earthworks, which had a representative serve on the advisory group, argued that FPIC should not be an optional process and that the Standard should explicitly require FPIC. The Earthworks submission said:

> "Obtaining Free, Prior and Informed Consent of Indigenous peoples for construction or expansion of tailings facilities must be moved from a footnote to a requirement."[15]

The Swiss Federal Agency for the Environment also commented on this issue. It said:

> "The Affected Communities section is welcome; it could perhaps be complemented (or introduced) with a reasoning using the internationally recognized 'free prior informed consent'."[16]

In the light of this feedback, the panel began revising the Standard to include FPIC as a standalone requirement. However, the ICMM was steadfastly opposed to a requirement that FPIC be *obtained*. It insisted that industry be required only to *work to obtain* such consent. This was the formulation used in its own position statement on Mining and Indigenous Peoples, which was adopted in 2013. That position statement required its corporate members to:

> "... *work to obtain* the consent of indigenous communities for new projects (and changes to existing projects) that are located on lands traditionally owned by or under customary use of indigenous peoples and are likely to have significant adverse impacts on indigenous peoples, including where relocation and/or significant adverse impacts on critical cultural heritage are likely to occur."[17]

This statement only requires companies to make an effort to obtain consent. It does not require that they abandon projects where consent is not forthcoming, or where conditions for proceeding with mining activities cannot be agreed. Thus, while the ICMM encourages its members to obtain FPIC to the greatest degree possible, it still leaves it up to each member company to decide whether to proceed in any specific circumstance.

In 2013, the position statement may have been a big step for the ICMM members. Seven years on, in 2020, the panel would have wanted to go beyond the ICMM position and to require that projects should not proceed unless FPIC had been obtained. However, the ICMM stipulated that the Standard must not go beyond its own position on this matter. It was made clear to the panel that the Council of mining company CEOs was not willing to re-open negotiations on the ICMM position statement as part of formulating the global industry Standard.

The Council of CEOs did, however, agree to one important addition to the wording. It is widely accepted that FPIC is not a one-off approval, but an ongoing process. The ICMM position statement and accompanying guidance describes FPIC as such. It is on this basis that the ICMM agreed to vary the wording to "work to obtain and

---

[15] Email responses, op cit, Earthworks, p 8.
[16] Email responses, op cit, Swiss Federal Agency for the Environment, p 2.
[17] ICMM, *Indigenous Peoples and Mining*. icmm.com/position-statements/indigenous-peoples.

maintain". This was not, as we learned later, well received by all ICMM members. Nonetheless, it was agreed to by the ICMM Secretariat during the drafting process.

The draft at this stage read as follows:

> "Where a new tailings facility may significantly impact the rights of indigenous or tribal peoples, including their land and resource rights and their right to self-determination, *work to obtain and maintain* Free, Prior and Informed Consent (FPIC)." (Emphasis added.)

Notice that the draft now requires FPIC only where impacts are *significant*, not for all impacts. This is wording from the industry's 2013 position statement (see above) and was one of the matters on which the ICMM was insisting.

This is the version that went to the 3 co-conveners on 10 March 2020 for their final consideration. A meeting to discuss the final draft was held on 18 May 2020, via Zoom, and included representatives from each of the co-convening organisations. UNEP and the PRI each had a small group of negotiators and the ICMM involved the CEOs from Anglo American, Antofagasta Minerals, Freeport-McMoRan, Glencore, Teck and Rio Tinto.

The word "significant" in the FPIC requirement was one of the last sticking points. UNEP insisted on its removal, it wanted all impacts to have FPIC not just significant ones. The ICMM CEOs refused. Several options were under consideration but nothing was agreed. Eventually at a second meeting on 27 May 2020, a compromise was proposed: the ICMM would accept the removal of the word "significant" if it could reference the ICMM position statement as meeting the requirement of the Standard. This was agreed. As a result, the requirement now read:

> "Where a new tailings facility may impact the rights of indigenous or tribal peoples, including their land and resource rights and their right to self-determination, work[18] to obtain and maintain Free Prior and Informed Consent (FPIC). *An Operator applying the ICMM position statement on Indigenous Peoples and Mining will be considered to meet this Requirement*." (Emphasis added.)

This was, in effect, a political compromise by the ICMM not a substantive one. UNEP achieved its lower threshold in the first sentence (the removal of "significant"). However, the ICMM position statement, *itself*, restricts FPIC to significant impacts. The second sentence meant, therefore, that operators need only consider obtaining FPIC for *significant* impacts. Clearly, the ICMM had out manoeuvred UNEP. The Standard was now all but finalised.

At this point events took a dramatic turn. The news arrived that, on 24 May 2020, Rio Tinto had blown up some ancient Aboriginal rock shelters ("caves" for short) in the Juukan Gorge of the Pilbara region of Western Australia, the heartland of Australia's mining iron ore industry, and that the traditional owners were devastated. Rio Tinto blasted the caves in order to expand one of its 16 iron ore mines. The company had, for some time, planned to expand its Brockman 4 mine and had consulted with traditional owners in the process, as required under national and state law.

In this case, the traditional owners and native title holders are the Puutu Kunti Kurrama and Pinikura People (PKKP). In Australia, native title holders have only

---

[18] For readers struggling to make grammatical sense of this quotation, note that "work" is an imperative.

limited rights to their land. Under native title law, exploration or mining activity triggers a "right to negotiate", which provides an opportunity for native title parties to negotiate agreements with project developers for access to their lands and territories.[19] These agreements can include conditions for conducting exploration or mining activities on traditional lands and provide certainty for mining companies in terms of land access. For traditional owners, these agreements provide guaranteed royalty streams in exchange for land access and enable their participation in land and cultural heritage management. In this sense, land access is supposed to be conditional on the active participation of traditional owners in the management of their land and cultural heritage.

Rio Tinto, the largest operator in the Pilbara, secured approval to destroy the rock shelters from the state of Western Australia in 2013. One of the conditions was to conduct archaeological excavations before destroying them. Archaeological studies conducted in 2014, with the participation of the traditional owners, found evidence of human occupation dating back 46,000 years. To put this into perspective, this is older than Stonehenge in England, the Pyramids of Egypt, the Colosseum in Italy and Machu Picchu in Peru. In one of the caves, archaeologists found grinding and pounding tools, sharpened marsupial bones and a 4,000-year-old belt made of human hair with DNA links of the PKKP peoples.

Having met the conditions of the state approval, Rio Tinto considered the caves ready for destruction. There was no appeal mechanism in the law allowing the PKKP to change the government's decision, despite new information about the staggering significance of the caves coming to light. In the land use agreement negotiated with Rio Tinto in 2011, the PKKP had relinquished their right to publicly challenge the company's cultural heritage decisions[20]. Breaching this agreement would compromise their benefit stream and give cause for Rio Tinto to bring legal action against them.

Things came to a head in the middle of May 2020. The PKKP requested access to the site for the upcoming Reconciliation Week – a nationally recognised week to celebrate indigenous history and culture in Australia and foster reconciliation discussion and activities. Rio Tinto said no, the traditional owners could not access the site because it was charged with explosives, which were about to be detonated. The PKKP asked Rio Tinto to remove the explosives and preserve the caves. Rio Tinto consulted blast experts but concluded that it was not safe to remove the charges[21]. On 24 May 2020, Rio Tinto exercised its legal right and destroyed the caves.

On 25 May, the PKKP Aboriginal Corporation released a statement, quoting the Puutu Kunti Kurrama Land Committee Chair:

> "Our people are deeply troubled and saddened by the destruction of these rock shelters and are grieving the loss of connection to our ancestors as well as our land ... Losing these rock shelters is a devastating blow to the PKKP Traditional Owners."[22]

---

[19] We note here that Australia's native title laws do not provide a power of "veto", but a limited "right to negotiate". Aboriginal Land Rights Act (Northern Territory) 1976 provides a stronger set of rights to content.

[20] These "gag clauses" are a common feature in Rio Tinto and other companies' agreements and a key issue to come to light in a public inquiry on the matter.

[21] A public inquiry has revealed that Rio Tinto continued to lay explosives after the PKKP's request to preserve the caves. abc.net.au/news/2020-10-16/rio-tinto-grilled-at-juukan-gorge-inquiry/12775866.

[22] BBC News, *Rio Tinto bosses lose bonuses over Aboriginal cave destruction*, 24 August 2020, bbc.com/news/business-53885695.

At risk of breaching their land use agreement, and in an unprecedented move, the PKKP had spoken out against Rio Tinto. They expressed publicly how distraught they were about the destruction of the caves. This occurred at the time of mass protests in the United States, following the shocking death of George Floyd at the hands of police. The Juukan Gorge cave destruction became an Australian Black Lives Matter issue. The public was incensed, and major investors became concerned that one of the industry's leaders could have committed such an act of "egregious vandalism".[23] The enormous power imbalance between companies and communities had been revealed, and Rio Tinto was accused of running roughshod over the wishes of traditional owners. This cultural catastrophe was happening just as the co-conveners were preparing to announce a new voluntary Standard on tailings management with the grand aspiration of zero harm to people and the environment.

The key point of contention in the Juukan Gorge case is whether or not the company had the consent of the PKKP for the destruction of the caves. In the days after the blast, a Puutu Kunti Kurrama spokesman said:

> "At all times the PKKPAC has been direct and explicit in the archaeological and ethnographic significance of these rock shelters and the importance that they be preserved."[24]

There was no question about the significance of the caves. The studies had been conducted, and the age of the caves was established. Rio Tinto claims to have obtained FPIC for mining in the area years earlier, initially via a Binding Initial Agreement in 2003 and later the 2011 land use agreement.[25] However, information about the significance of the caves came to light after these agreements were struck, and circumstances changed. This meant that consent was no longer operative, as far as the traditional owners were concerned. Rio Tinto was either unaware or chose to overlook these changes. From this point of view, Rio Tinto had not maintained the PKKP's consent for its mining activities.[26]

As details emerged of what had happened in the Pilbara, the Global Tailings Review (GTR) process almost unravelled. UNEP wrote to the other co-conveners indicating that it was stepping away from the process. It wanted to distance itself from the industry at this time. As the expert panel was not part of these exchanges, we do not know how close the process came to falling over. The withdrawal of UNEP, and a disintegration of the process, would have been devastating for everyone involved – and everyone who was hopeful of achieving a step-change in industry practice on tailings facility management.

---

[23] Langton, M, We need a thorough investigation into the destruction of the Juukan Gorge caves. A mere apology will not cut it, *The Guardian*, 28 July 2020: theguardian.com/commentisfree/2020/jul/28/we-need-a-thorough-investigation-into-the-destruction-of-the-juukan-gorge-caves-a-mere-apology-will-not-cut-it.

[24] Myles, C, Rio Tinto knew of 46,000-year-old Pilbara site's significance 'as recently as March', traditional owners say, WAtoday, 31 May 2020. watoday.com.au/national/western-australia/rio-tinto-knew-of-46-000-year-old-pilbara-site-s-significance-as-recently-as-march-traditional-owners-say-20200530-p54xyt.html.

[25] See Rio Tinto's submission to the Joint Standing Committee Inquiry into the destruction of 46,000 year old caves at the Juukan Gorge in the Pilbara region of Western Australia: aph.gov.au/Parliamentary_Business/Committees/Joint/Northern_Australia/CavesatJuukanGorge/Submissions. Submission no 25.

[26] Submissions and testimony provided to a public inquiry later revealed that Rio Tinto's actions violated key tenets of FPIC.

Eventually, through a series of urgent and confidential discussions between the parties, UNEP agreed to re-join negotiations, on the condition that the ICMM accepted its proposal for the FPIC requirement, without further discussion. The word "significant" was deleted, and reference to the ICMM position statement removed. In the final Standard, the requirement reads as follows:

> "Where a new tailings facility may impact the rights of indigenous or tribal peoples, including their land and resource rights and their right to self-determination, work to obtain and maintain Free Prior and Informed Consent (FPIC) by demonstrating conformance to international guidance and recognised best practice frameworks."

As can be seen in the wording above, UNEP had also insisted on one other change, substitution of the reference to the ICMM position statement with the phrase "by demonstrating conformance to international guidance and recognised best practice frameworks". In practical terms, it may appear that the ICMM lost nothing here. A mining company could easily argue that the ICMM's position statement on Mining and Indigenous Peoples amounts to the international guidance specified in this formulation. This would enable a company to restrict FPIC to significant impacts only. However, the change also leaves the door open for application of *stronger* guidance – if an independent entity deems that the ICMM position statement does not go far enough. The impact of this change will only be seen as the implementation process plays out over time.

On this occasion, then, the ICMM CEOs did not entirely get their way. But it had taken a catastrophe for them to back down. Even so, the final wording of the requirement retains much of the ICMM's original wording preferences, such as "*work* to obtain". Moreover, in the absence of an independent entity (see Chapter 11), the wording is vague enough for the ICMM to be able to claim that compliance with its own position statement satisfies the requirement.

Concluding comments

To summarise, the ICMM member companies pushed back on the inclusion of social aspects through the whole process, arguing that tailings facility management was a technical arena and that a global Standard should not be congested with non-technical considerations. The ICMM CEOs explicitly wound back requirements for operators to listen to project-affected peoples. They very determinedly sought to remove the possibility for other parties to share any real power in the process of tailings facility management.

Part of the reason for this intransigence was that the ICMM CEOs and their technical advisors were largely unaware of the details of various international instruments that their companies had endorsed, and of the implications these instruments had for dealings with affected communities on project-related matters. The ICMM member companies employ specialists in social and environmental performance who would have been able to educate CEOs and their technical advisors about issues such as participation, human rights and consent. Yet the CEOs failed to draw these specialists into the GTR process in a formal way. The expert panel sought the formal engagement of these specialists, just as the industry's tailings specialists had been engaged. This never eventuated. It was almost as if the company social and environmental specialists had been banned from formal participation. The result was that the panel had to undertake the task of educating parts of the ICMM member companies about their own commitments in relation to social performance, needlessly prolonging the debates on these issues.

The sidelining of social performance expertise is a broader phenomenon that one of us (Kemp) has written about for more than a decade. It is a key factor that enabled Rio Tinto to knowingly destroy the Juukan Gorge rock shelters without any awareness by its senior management of what was occurring. If traditional owners themselves had been listened to, and industry social performance specialists had had the influence or authority to intervene, this may never have happened. We take up this question again in Chapter 8.

The whole process revealed to us how far removed some of the industry's leaders are from the current political milieu, and the rapidly evolving frameworks of participation, human rights and consent. This lack of openness, adaptability and willingness to listen, and to share power, goes to the heart of the politics embedded in the GTR process. It is also symptomatic of the arrangements that underpin the way the industry operates.

CHAPTER 8

Accountability and governance

The Standard should clearly specify that accountability for tailings dam safety sits with the board of the corporation. This comment was made frequently during the public consultation on the Standard.[1]

However, the final Standard does not mention board accountability, for which it has been repeatedly criticised. This chapter:

■ explains why the Standard does not require board accountability

■ outlines a way in which a board can structure accountability for safety into a mining company's processes

■ shows how this can be extended to cover social and environmental performance

■ considers the extent to which the Standard measures up to this ideal and explains why it falls short.

Tailings facility failure is one of the several types of major accidents that can befall mining companies. Others include high-wall collapses in open cut pits, explosions in underground coal mines and explosions in mineral processing plants. Accountability must cover all these possibilities. For this reason, the discussion here is generalised to major accidents, not just tailings facility failures. At some points we generalise even further, to sustainability.

Board accountability

Any discussion of accountability must begin by clarifying what it means. Holding a person or entity accountable means requiring that they give an account, that is, an explanation. It also must include the possibility of imposing consequences, where the account is found to be unsatisfactory.[2] To speak of accountability, we must be able to answer the following 3 questions:

■ Accountable **to** whom?

■ Accountable **for** what?

■ How is the accountable person or entity **held to account**?

In relation to boards, there are 2 main kinds of accountability – legal accountability and accountability to shareholders.[3] First, in many jurisdictions, boards are accountable **to** the courts, **for** compliance with various regulations, but rarely are

---

[1] Email responses, op cit, Earthworks, pp 5, 56, 79, 85.

[2] Keay, AR and Loughrey, J, The framework for board accountability in corporate governance, *Legal Studies* 2015, 35 (2) pp: 252–279.

[3] There are others. See Hopkins, A, Addressing the organisational weaknesses that contribute to disaster, *GTR Compendium*, Chapter X, p 183. globaltailingsreview.org/wp-content/uploads/2020/09/Ch-X-Addressing-the-Organisational-Weaknesses-that-Contribute-to-Disaster.pdf.

they **held to account**, meaning that this is seldom an effective form of accountability. Second, boards are accountable to shareholders **for**, among other things, generating acceptable shareholder returns, and are **held to account**, sometimes, at shareholder meetings. If boards are held to account by their shareholders only after a major accident that affects shareholder returns, this will be a relatively ineffective form of accountability since such accidents are rare within any one company. On the other hand, if shareholders hold their boards to account for managing major accident risks on a more regular basis, this can be an effective form of accountability. Shareholders are increasingly looking for ways to hold boards accountable for the ongoing management of major accident risks, especially in relation to tailings facilities, in the case of the mining industry.

A third type of accountability that is sometimes mentioned in this context is accountability to the public – public accountability. But this is seldom an effective form of accountability since there are few mechanisms by which the public can hold boards to account. The exception is when the actions or inactions of a board have created such a public outrage that shareholders and/or governments are motivated to take action.

One way that boards can respond to the possibility of being held to account is to appoint at least one board member who has expertise in the relevant major accident risks. In the petrochemical industry, stakeholders in the United Kingdom (UK) have signed up to a set of "process safety principles". (Process safety is the term used in this industry to refer to major accident risks, such as the risk of gas explosions.) One of these principles reads as follows:

> "At least one board member should be fully conversant in process safety management in order to advise the board of the status of process safety risk management within the organization and of the process safety implications of board decisions."[4]

This principle could easily be applied to mining companies. A board that includes one or more experts in major accident risks in the mining sector is in a good position to reach down into the organisation and ask intelligent and probing questions about how risks are being managed. Inquiries into major accidents frequently find that people at the workface were aware that risks were not being adequately managed, but that this information was not passed up the organisational hierarchy. It is important that boards are sensitive to this possibility and have some independent capacity to seek out "bad news" of this type. Such a board is better able to provide an account of how the company is managing major accident risks if called upon to do so.

Some companies have established sub-committees of their boards to focus more widely on environment, health and safety, the well-being of mining-affected communities and other social obligations. These are variously called sustainability committees or corporate responsibility committees. We should caution that these sub-committees only work effectively if board members with special responsibility for keeping their boards informed are willing to bypass senior executives and reach down into the organisation to find out for themselves what is going on. If the Board of Rio Tinto had asked more probing questions about how their company was managing

---

[4] UK Health and Safety Executive (n.d.) PSLG Principles of Process Safety Leadership, UK HSE, (n.d.) www.hse.gov.uk/comah/buncefield/pslgprinciples.pdf; See also www.hse.gov.uk/comah/guidance/major-hazard-leadership-intervention-tool.pdf.

its relations with indigenous peoples in Western Australia, the company might not have gone ahead with its disastrous plan to destroy the Juukan Gorge caves.

There is a widespread view that the more serious the possible consequences of a risk decision, the higher in the corporation that decision should be made. Where the potential consequences are catastrophic, threatening the survival of the corporation in its existing form, it should be the board that makes the final decision. Of course, boards will be advised by the company specialists. But boards may take a broader view than these experts. In particular, they may give greater weight to the reputational damage that a catastrophic failure could cause, even though the likelihood of such a failure might be extremely remote. A board member or members with specialist knowledge about the major accident risks faced by the corporation can greatly assist this process. As one investor said during the consultation process for the Standard:

> "We want to know that oversight and decision making for these high consequence, material risks resides at the highest level of the company, where our Board nominees can have influence, or at very least be aware of status, and where decisions are less susceptible to the internal corporate influences that executives can be exposed to."[5]

The idea that boards might be involved in such decision-making is sometimes opposed on the grounds that this inappropriately blurs the line between boards and executive managers. A board's role, according to this argument, should be to ensure that there are systems in place to manage risk and that these systems are properly audited, but not to inquire too deeply into how these risks are being managed, or get involved in particular decisions because this infringes on the role of senior management. However, this is too rigid a view. Where risks can have material consequences, that is, can significantly affect the share value, it is ultimately the responsibility of the board to decide whether, or on what basis, to accept the risk. This principle is well understood in the case of purely financial decisions, such as mergers and acquisitions. It should also be the case in relation to major accident risks, which can materially affect the business. There is not and cannot be a rigid line between the board and the executive in this matter.

All this leads to some important conclusions. We agree with the submissions made during the public consultation that boards should be held accountable for major accident risk and for sustainability more generally,[6] but this will only happen if there are persons or entities able to hold them to account. This can most easily be done by shareholders and/or the courts. The Standard is a list of requirements that *mining companies* must comply with, if they seek to have their tailings facilities certified (more on certification in Chapter 11). It cannot impose requirements on governments or shareholders to hold boards accountable. For this reason, the Standard is silent on the accountability of boards.

On the other hand, members of the expert panel *recommend* board accountability in a volume that accompanies the Standard, the *GTR compendium*. In particular, one of us (Hopkins) urged that "shareholders should hold boards accountable for the ongoing management of major accident risks".[7] Another panel member advocated in the *compendium* that governments should impose legal liability on corporate directors.[8]

---

5   Email responses, op cit, Principles for Responsible Investment, p 12.
6   See footnote 1.
7   Hopkins, A, op cit, p vi.
8   Squillace, M, "The Role of the State", *The GTR Compendium*, Chapter XII, p 168.

The need for specialised accountability mechanisms to counteract production pressures

If a board is seeking to prevent major accidents, an obvious way to do this is to hold the CEO accountable for managing these risks. But this is not enough. CEOs are also accountable to boards for commercial performance, which is normally the primary concern. This concern is transmitted down through the company with the result that, at all levels, commercial considerations are likely to take precedence over the effective management of major accident risk, unless there are strong countervailing mechanisms. We sketch some proposed countervailing mechanisms in the next section of this chapter. But before doing that, we describe 2 particular sources of the overwhelming production pressures that operate in mining companies and show how these pressures can contribute to major accidents. The first source of pressure is the production forecasts that companies provide to stock exchanges. The second is the production bonuses that are paid to senior managers and, in particular, top executives. This discussion is to some extent a detour from the issue of accountability, but it aims to show just how powerful these production pressures are, and hence how important it is to have accountability mechanisms that can effectively counterbalance them. Box 8.1 is a case study in which a production forecast or "market guidance" provided to the stock exchange led ultimately to a major accident.

Box 8.1: How share market guidance led to a major accident

A metalliferous (hard rock) mine suffered a major underground rock fall. No one was killed or injured, but mining was interrupted for months, which cost the company dearly. Accordingly, the company set up a high-powered incident investigation team to understand what had gone wrong.

The team identified "market guidance" as one of the critical issues. To understand how this worked requires some additional background. Mining companies routinely issue reports to stock exchanges providing "best estimates" of production for some upcoming period, for example the remainder of the financial year. The estimates are not intended to be firm predictions. As one stock exchange states, "It is the single most realistic assessment of recoverable quantities, if only a single result were reported. Where probabilistic methods are used, there should be a 50% probability [P50] that the quantities actually recovered will be equal to or exceed the best estimate." That means of course there will be a 50% probability that the quantity actually recovered will be *less than* the best estimate.

However, best estimates are distorted in at least 2 ways. First, companies tend to overestimate how much they will produce – a classic optimism bias. Second, once the best estimate is announced to the stock exchange it becomes, for all concerned, a target that must be reached. Failure to meet the target is seen as a failure to live up to market guidance and could have a detrimental effect on share prices. As explained above, that is not the true meaning or intention of market guidance, but it is the way it is interpreted in practice. This is critical to understanding the way in which market guidance becomes a source of production pressure.

In the present case, as mining progressed, conditions were becoming ever more challenging and it was becoming increasingly difficult to maintain the rate of production specified in the market guidance of the previous year. The report states:

> "it was noted through the investigation interviews that key individuals at the site are feeling the pressure of achieving the market guidance ... there are definite signs at the operation that it is under stress trying to meet the market guidance".

It was in response to these pressures that the mine's planners chose a particular mining sequence that led ultimately to failure.

Consider now the situation of the mine's geotechnical specialists. It was their job to keep the mine safe. Even more, as someone said, it was their job to keep the managers out of jail. The head geo-technician had felt uneasy about the mining plan being followed. "If I'd had my way", he told the inquiry, "I would have changed the mining sequence". He had a "gut feeling", he said, that the proposed sequence was not sound. His concern was based on geotechnical experience, but not hard data – professional judgements about risk seldom are. This meant that he was easily overridden.

The inquiry asked his boss why he had not paid greater attention to the geotech's concerns. His response was that he "could not talk to the business on the basis of a gut feeling".

It is clear, however, that the concern of the head geotechnical specialist would have been more difficult to ignore if he had been higher in the organisational structure, in particular, if he had outranked, or even been on a par with the planners.

Indeed, given the right organisational structure, he would have been in a position to veto the proposed mining sequence. The report concluded as follows:

"The influence of the geotechnical function needs to be strengthened: the investigation team identified through numerous interviews that the geotechnical team's voice is not strong enough and that their concerns are diluted under the production pressures and priorities" (emphasis in the original).

We draw 2 conclusions from this case. First, market guidance can produce powerful production pressures that can lead ultimately to a major accident. Second, those charged with ensuring the technical integrity of mining operations must have real organisational power, if they are to stand any chance of resisting these pressures.

Inquiries into tailings dam failures seldom investigate whether market guidance was a contributing factor. However, wherever such guidance or targets exist, it is a reasonable assumption that they contribute to the prioritisation of production over safety that has characterised recent tailings dam failures. It is notable that both Vale and Imperial Metals (the owner of the Mount Polley mine that suffered a tailings dam failure in 2014) were providing market guidance to the stock exchanges on which they were listed.

Bonuses are the second mechanism we have singled out as generating production pressures that can lead to accidents. In Box 8.2 we describe this mechanism in more detail.

Box 8.2: How bonuses create production pressures and contribute to major accidents[9]

In the corporate world, bonuses or incentive payments are a ubiquitous accountability mechanism by which boards ensure their senior executives act in accordance with shareholder interests, generally understood to mean maximising shareholder returns. These incentives cascade down to relatively junior managers and agents. A great deal of evidence in the banking industry shows that such bonuses are highly effective in

---

[9] This box draws on Hopkins, A and Maslen, S, (2015), *Risky Rewards: How Company Bonuses Affect Safety.* Burlington 2015, VT: Ashgate Publishing Company. ebookcentral-proquest-com.ezproxy. library.uq.edu.au/lib/uql/detail.action?docID=1897140.

maximising shareholder returns in the short term, but have also led to excessive risk-taking that can end in financial and reputational crisis for all concerned. The global financial crisis of 2008 is perhaps the best known of these crises, but there are many others.

In the mining industry, annual incentive payments to mine managers and to employees are largely centred on production — tonnes produced. There are targets and even stretch targets, which, if reached, trigger higher payments. There may also be additional bonus payments for managers who are able to bring new operations into production earlier than scheduled. In this way, bonuses contribute powerfully to production pressures.

Typically, however, some portion of the annual bonus paid to senior managers is dependent on safety performance, measured primarily by workforce injury rate. This provides an incentive to improve safety. Unfortunately, it also provides an incentive to suppress reporting and to reclassify injuries to minimise their significance. These unintended consequences are well known, but we disregard them for present purposes. The safety component of bonuses typically accounts for a much smaller proportion of the total bonus than production, but it is reasonable to conclude that it has some beneficial effect on safety.

However, linking bonuses to injury rates is irrelevant when it comes to the management of major accident risk. Major accidents are rare in the life of any one mine and may even be rare in the life of a large mining company. As a result, they do not contribute to the annual injury rate. Incentivising the reduction in injury rates therefore does nothing to incentivise better management of major accident risks. Indeed, from a cynical point of view, most managers can afford to pay little attention to major accident risks, on the grounds that they are most unlikely to experience a major accident on their watch in the facility or facilities under their control. Moreover, the fact that a facility or company may go for many years without a major accident means that the defects in major accident risk management remain hidden from view until an accident finally happens, at which time those defects become painfully obvious. The underground coal mine explosion at Moura in Queensland in 1994 provides a vivid case study of how incentive payments for production and for the reduction of injury rates leads to systematic neglect of major accident risks.[10]

In addition to these annual bonuses, the most senior executives of big companies, and mining companies in particular, receive so-called "long-term" bonuses. These are provisionally allocated each year based on various factors, which may include injury rates. They become due for payment some years later, typically 3, but whether they are actually paid (vest) depends *entirely* on share market performance in the interim period. This provides a steady pressure on senior executives to focus on shareholder returns above all else. Moreover, there is a particular mechanism that sharpens this pressure. Payment of the bonus depends on the share market performance of the company *relative* to a selected group of competitor companies. In the case of Vale, to take one example, its comparator group consists of Anglo-American, BHP, Freeport, Glencoe, Rio Tinto, Alcoa and South 32.[11] If the company falls into the lowest quartile of this group, the long-term bonus is wiped out. For higher quartiles, the amount paid depends on exactly where the company sits in ranking with respect to total shareholder returns. Putting it bluntly, this provides continuous pressure on top executives to keep up with or get ahead of the pack.

Tailings facilities are expensive to construct and operate safely. One way mining companies can augment total shareholder returns and hence the value of the long-term bonus is to

---

[10] Hopkins, A, *Managing Major Mazards: The Lessons of the Moura Mine Disaster*, Allen and Unwin, Sydney, 1999.
[11] www.vale.com/esg/en/Pages/Compensation.aspx.

> minimise expenditure on these facilities. The result is that the long-term bonus systems are potentially detrimental to tailings facility safety. Some companies make provision to "claw back" these long-term bonuses in the rare event of a major accident that does real damage to the company. But precisely because this is a rare event, such a possibility does little to counteract the continuous pressure to overlook major accident risks that a long-term bonus system exerts.

An accountable executive

The preceding discussion has demonstrated the power of the production imperative and the need for equally powerful countervailing mechanisms to ensure that major accident risks are properly managed. Mining companies sometimes designate a senior executive, called an *accountable executive,* to perform this function. The use of this term is not restricted to the mining industry and its meaning varies with the context. Some of the matters that depend on that context are who may be appointed an accountable executive, to whom the appointee is accountable, for what they are accountable and by what mechanism they might be held to account. In what follows, we define from first principles an ideal role for an accountable executive in the mining industry. We shall also discuss the extent to which the requirements of the Standard measure up to this ideal.

As discussed above, there is an inevitable tension between production, on one hand, and safety, or risk control, on the other. It is important that this tension be manifested at the highest level of the corporation, with these 2 goals championed to varying degrees by different people. In situations where chief operating officers and business unit leaders may tend to give greater emphasis to production or profit, an accountable executive must be able to argue unequivocally for safety. Where there are significant differences of opinion, it will be the CEO who makes the decision, but with the benefit of hearing the arguments on both sides. For this arrangement to be effective, the accountable executive must have the same status as those on the other side of the debate, which means that if they report directly to the CEO, so must the accountable executive. Without an accountable executive operating in this way, the tension between production and safety is buried and resolved at lower levels of the organisation, too often in favour of production.

Furthermore, given earlier observations about boards, directors need to be able to see the tensions in the organisation and satisfy themselves that the management is dealing properly with the trade-offs between these somewhat competing objectives.[12] This requires a direct line of communication between the accountable executive and the board. The accountable executive must be able to raise issues in a timely manner, not restricted to scheduled quarterly or annual reporting and not subject to any restrictions or oversight by the CEO. This executive, therefore, has dual reporting lines, to both the CEO and the board. To maximise the autonomy of the position,

---

[12] ICOLD (2017). *Dam Safety Management: Operational Phase of the Dam Life Cycle, Bulletin* #154. Paris: International Commission on Large Dams. www.ussdams.org/wpcontent/uploads/2016/04/B154. pdf, pp 55, 77.
[13] The Mining Association of Canada's *Guide to the Management of Tailings Facilities* (MAC 2019) envisages that the Accountable Executive will be "designated" by the board. www.mining.ca/documents/a-guide-to-the-management-of-tailings-facilities-version-3-1-2019/.

the appointment should be made or confirmed by the board.[13] In the final analysis, therefore, the accountable executive is accountable to the board.

It is clear from this discussion that the accountable executive cannot be anyone who has production responsibilities or targets. This should be no barrier to identifying an appropriate person because companies often have a chief sustainability officer, or a chief risk officer, or an executive manager for health and safety or for safety and major accident risk. As long as such people report to the CEO, and are ultimately accountable to the board, they can fulfil the role of the accountable executive described above.

Finally, there is the question of what the accountable executive is accountable for. In principle, the role is to ensure that proper attention is paid to risk management and compliance throughout the corporation. Given the breadth of this role, there will need to be a structure of positions subordinate to the accountable executive to which the responsibilities of the role are delegated. We distinguish here between accountability and responsibility.[14] The meaning of accountability was discussed at the start of this chapter. On the other hand, responsibility in the present context means, roughly, job. So here we are saying that the accountable executive may delegate jobs. The person to whom the responsibility is delegated becomes accountable to the executive for the performance of the job, and the executive remains accountable to the board for the performance of the subordinate. More on this below.

The Standard

The preceding ideas were included in early drafts of the Standard. However, even before the Standard went out for public consultation, the International Council for Mining and Metals (ICMM) CEOs had insisted that the requirements relating to the accountable executive be modified (see discussion of "powerplay" in Chapter 4). This executive was no longer to report to the CEO, but simply a member of "senior management". And no longer was the position to be accountable to the board. The consultation feedback on this point strengthened the expert panel's resolve and the ICMM's changes were reversed in the version of the Standard that went to the co-conveners for their final consideration. The accountable executive was again to report directly to the CEO. But during the final negotiations the ICMM re-asserted its position. As a result, the requirement in the ultimate version began as follows:

> "Appoint one or more Accountable Executives who is/are directly answerable to the CEO on matters related to this Standard."

At first sight, this is a strange proposal. It was designed to accommodate a few CEOs who did not want to have the accountable executive as a direct report. The rationale was as follows. To be "answerable to the CEO on matters related to this Standard" meant that on other matters this executive would *not* be answerable to the CEO. In fact, the accountable executive would need to report (in the usual sense) to someone

---

[14] For a more extensive discussion see Hopkins, A, *Failure to Learn: The BP Texas City Refinery Disaster.* CCH Sydney, 2008, pp 131–133.

else, at a lower level than the CEO. Given our earlier analysis, this could be expected to inhibit communication with the CEO.

One can assume that the intention of the objectors was to avoid having to make any changes in their organisational structure. The responsibilities of the accountable executive would be grafted onto an existing position within each of the constituent businesses. If those existing positions had any responsibility for profit or production, this would almost certainly compromise the accountable executive function, but there is no hint of any such concern in the final wording.

Interestingly, some of the expert panel's original wording remained in the final version. This requires that the multiple accountable executives have regular communication with the board of directors and that the board should demonstrate how it holds these multiple executives accountable. This is an unwieldy outcome and probably an unintended consequence of the final negotiation process.

The accountability of mining and geotechnical engineers

The role of accountable executives provides a solution to the problem faced by technical experts at lower levels in the organisational structure. Recall that the geotechnical specialist in Box 8.1 lacked the authority − organisational clout − to insist on good mining practice. Similarly, tailings facility engineers, subject to budgetary constraints imposed on them by the mine where they work, may not be able to insist on good engineering practice.

The solution is that such engineers should have dual reporting lines, a primary line that culminates with the accountable executive and a secondary reporting line to the local site manager. Provided the company maintains this primary/secondary distinction, this will ensure that safety and facility integrity take precedence over production. In terms of organisational charts, this can be represented as a solid reporting line that culminates with the accountable executive and a dotted reporting line to the site manager (see Figure 8.1 below). Note that this is the reverse of the more common situation where the primary reporting line is within the business unit, with a dotted line to an external technical specialist at the corporate level. The arrangement described here protects technical specialists from undue commercial pressures from mine management that might otherwise result in decisions that are undesirable from a safety point of view. Of course, there will need to be co-ordination between the immediate supervisor in the business unit and the supervisor in the line to the accountable executive, but these matters are not difficult to resolve.

The critical feature of this organisational design is that the technical specialist has a performance agreement with a supervisor in the line reporting to the accountable executive. This agreement will naturally give priority to safety and technical integrity. The annual performance assessment of the technical specialist will be based on this performance agreement. This means that the technical specialist is accountable, ultimately, to the accountable executive and not to a local business or mine manager. This would have resolved the problem faced by the geotechnical specialist in Box 8.1; it would also empower tailings engineers to insist on good practice.

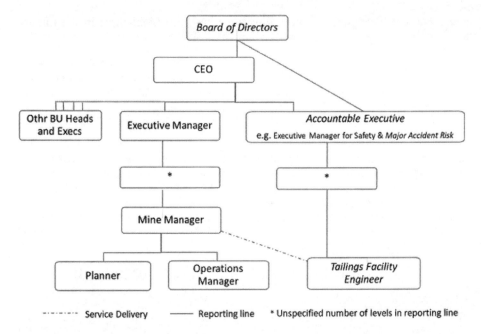

Figure 8.1: Skeletal organisational chart showing relationships referred to in the text

There are many examples of companies in hazardous industries operating with a dual reporting structure of the type described here. An outstanding example is BP as it was re-organised after the Gulf of Mexico blowout in 2010.[15] BP's engineers report primarily up an engineering line that culminates several steps above site level in a global head (although not one answering directly to the CEO). Moreover, BP has a safety and operational risk function with a head answering to the CEO and with staff embedded in local business units, both providing risk management services and ensuring compliance. This approach seems less common in the mining industry, but arguably, disasters such as the Brumadinho tailings dam failure will drive the industry in this direction.

The Standard

These ideas were incorporated in the draft of the Standard put out for consultation. However, the ICMM categorically rejected the whole idea of dual reporting lines for a tailings facility engineer, and particularly the idea that the primary line should be to the accountable executive. It agreed only that there should be "regular communication with the accountable executive", which became the wording in the final version of the Standard. This substantially weakened the ability of the engineer to put the integrity of the facility ahead of cost.

Appropriate financial incentives

Given the tension between short-term profit maximisation and longer-term risk control, any system that incentivises commercial success is inappropriate for people

---

[15] Hopkins A, *Organising for Safety: How Structure Creates Culture*, CCH, Sydney, 2019.

whose primary task is risk control. This issue has been highlighted in the finance industry. Many banks have a chief risk officer (CRO) who is part of the executive team, answerable directly to the CEO. Reports into recent banking scandals demonstrate that the CRO in these cases had not carried out the responsibilities of the role effectively, in part because the incentive payments available to this officer prioritised annual profit, rather than risk control.

A much-quoted guidance document for the finance sector in the UK gives the following advice:

> "Staff engaged in financial and risk control should be compensated in a manner that is independent of the business areas they oversee and commensurate with their key role in the firm."[16]

These ideas are equally applicable to the management of major accident risk in the mining sector. The direct implication is that neither the accountable executive nor the staff in that function should be incentivised in relation to production, profit or cost reduction. The simplest way to achieve this outcome is to pay them a fixed salary, augmented, if necessary, to compensate for the fact that they are not eligible for bonuses. Alternatively, if it is important to pay them bonuses, they can be incentivised on the basis of how well they perform in relation to their job specification or performance agreement. This can be based on judgements made by a supervisor at the time of a performance review. These conclusions apply also to engineers and technical specialists whose primary reporting line culminates in the accountable executive.

For employees whose primary role is to contribute to production or cost reduction, albeit safely, the implications are different. Presumably, the major component of their bonuses will be based on production and cost reduction, but there should also be a component based on safety or integrity. However, it is a mistake to base this component on quantitative metrics such as injury rates. This leads almost inevitably to attempts to manage the metric, rather than the risk, as mentioned earlier. This problem can be overcome if bonuses are based on qualitative judgements about the employee's contribution to safety and operational integrity. It will be up to the employee to make this case during performance reviews. This will provide a strong incentive for employees to take these matters into account.

One of the most effective ways that production-oriented employees can also contribute to safety is by reporting problems that they become aware of in their normal duties. Companies should incentivise such reporting. They need not reward people each and every time they speak up, as this runs the risk of generating a large number of trivial reports. Rather, they should offer periodic rewards or awards for the best or most helpful reports at each site. That will encourage the reporting of whatever it is that site management finds most helpful. Award winners should be publicly recognised, preferably with a material reward, and with a clear explanation of how their contribution resulted in safer facility management.[17]

Consider, finally, the issue of long-term bonuses, discussed in Box 8.2. The banking industry is leading the way towards solutions here. Nowadays it is

---

[16] UK Financial Stability Forum (FSF), *Principles for Sound Compensation Practice*, 2009, p 7. www.fsb. org/wp-content/uploads/r_0904b.pdf.

[17] For a more extensive discussion of how this works, see Hopkins 2019, op cit, pp 127–135.

commonplace in the UK banking sector for long-term bonuses to include consideration of non-financial performance.[18] In Australia, the regulator is proposing to limit to 50% the contribution of financial metrics to such bonuses.[19] The remaining 50% would be made up of considerations such as effectiveness and operation of control and compliance, customer outcomes, market integrity objectives and reputation.

In the mining industry, the relevant non-financial considerations would include how well the company was managing catastrophic risk. This is not a simple matter and companies will need to innovate. It will be important that they are transparent about how they do this.

The Standard

An early draft of the Standard contained requirements embodying these ideas about bonuses. But these were largely lost in the initial intervention by the ICMM CEOs.[20] As a result, the consultation draft included only a modest requirement along these lines:

> "For employees who have a role in the tailings management system, *consider implementing* a performance incentive program to *include* a component linked to the integrity of tailings facilities." (Italics added.)

Even this was too much for the ICMM. Its response was blunt:

> "The Standard must refrain from setting requirements for remuneration, compensation or bonuses for various personnel."[21]

The reasons given for this outright rejection were unconvincing and it is clear that the panel had strayed into territory in which companies were simply unwilling to be told what to do.

However, both the United Nations Environment Program (UNEP) and the Principles for Responsible Investment (PRI) wanted this requirement strengthened. This is one matter on which they carried the day. Accordingly, the final version retains the logic sketched earlier in this section. Recommendation 8.3 reads as follows:

> "For roles with responsibility for tailings facilities, develop mechanisms such that incentive payments or performance reviews are based, at least in part, on public safety and the integrity of the tailings facility. These incentive payments shall reflect the degree to which public safety and the integrity of the tailings facility are part of the role. Long-term incentives for relevant executive managers should take tailings management into account."

This is one of the undoubted step changes in the Standard. We wait with bated breath to see how this requirement is implemented.

---

[18] APRA, *Discussion Paper: Strengthening Prudential Requirements for Remuneration*, Australian Prudential Regulatory Authority 23 July 2019, p 32. www.apra.gov.au/sites/default/files/discussion_paper_strengthening_prudential_requirements_for_remuneration_july_2019_v1.pdf.
[19] APRA, op cit, p 31.
[20] See "powerplay" described in Chapter 4.
[21] Email responses, op cit, ICMM, p 16.

Social and environmental performance

Production pressure can lead to bad outcomes for local communities and for the environment, quite apart from tailings facility failure. These more general social and environmental outcomes are the subject of this section. We argue that the accountability mechanisms for the management of major accident risk should be adopted for managing social and environmental performance more generally. We begin this section with a vignette that demonstrates the issue.

Box 8.3: The failure of a grievance mechanism to protect the interests of ethnic minorities[22]

The mine was located in an area occupied by ethnic minorities. As the mine expanded, its land access unit needed to negotiate with local landowners for new land in return for cash compensation. Production pressures meant these negotiations were often rushed and unsatisfactory from the point of view of local landowners, giving rise to numerous grievances.

The mine operated a grievance unit with 5 locally engaged staff, located in a community relations department on site. This unit had very little influence at the mine site and often had difficulty getting other mine departments, such as the land access unit, to engage with complainants on the grounds that they were too busy. The grievance unit was able to escalate matters to the site-level community relations manager and the mine manager, but both of these people had other priorities when it came to dealing with landowner grievances. Sometimes, the company's external affairs team in the capital of the country in which the mine was located played a role in handling local grievances. However, this team was primarily responsible for managing political affairs in the capital, which meant it too was compromised. Importantly, the grievance unit had no line of communication or appeal to higher levels in the parent company. It was an organisational orphan. The company policy was that unsatisfied complainants needed to take their grievance to external local government authorities. The problem here was that the local government viewed the mine as a nation-building project and treated the opposition as tantamount to acting against the national interest. If complainants did not accept whatever was on offer, they ran the risk of being detained by the state, possibly for years. In short, the avenues available to complainants outside the company were largely ineffective.[23]

Part of the problem outlined in Box 8.3 is that the grievance unit was located in a community relations department. The role of this department was to manage community relations in the interests of the company and the state, not necessarily in the interests of the community. Grievance mechanisms will predictably be ineffective in this situation. To overcome this problem, the grievance unit must have access to higher levels of the company via a social and environmental performance function that can bypass local mine management. This function must be set up with the purpose of securing good social and environmental performance, not with the purpose of smoothing the way for the company to maximise production.

---

[22] Owen, J and Kemp, D, *Extractive Relations: Countervailing Power and the Global Mining Industry*, Abingdon, Oxon 2017; New York, NY: Routledge, Chapter 11.

[23] Another extreme example of what can happen without an effective grievance mechanism unfolded at the Ok Tedi mine in Papua New Guinea in the 1980s when, with the permission of the government, the company discharged its tailings into the river over a long period, doing major environmental damage to the river all the way to the sea and destroying the livelihood of thousands of villagers.

To be fully effective, this social and environmental performance function must be embedded at sites, and report up a line that culminates in a position on the executive committee, exactly as is required for the management of major accident risks. Moreover, good social and environmental performance is not in tension with major accident risk management, as it is with production. It is complementary. One possibility might therefore be to combine the roles of executive managers for major accident risk and social and environmental performance into one position, perhaps titled executive manager for sustainability.

One of us (Kemp) has previously stressed the importance of countervailing force to ensure that the production imperative does not ride roughshod over the interests of the local people and the environment.[24] A social and environmental performance function culminating on the executive committee is one way of achieving this objective.

Just as we were writing these words, the review by Rio Tinto's board into the Juukan Gorge rock shelter fiasco appeared.[25] The board's response exemplifies nearly all the organisational principles advocated in this chapter. First, it announces that a social performance function will be established that culminates in, reports to, an executive on the Rio Tinto executive committee. Second, it specifies that this position is also the culmination point for the health, safety and environment function, as well as technical and projects. In our view, the inclusion of "projects" is undesirable, since that role is likely to be production oriented. This conflicts with the thrust of the health, safety and environment and social performance roles that aim to ensure that these issues are not sacrificed in the interests of production. But otherwise, the position looks very like that of the accountable executive in Figure 8.1.

Third, as well as being part of a specialised function that reports up to the executive committee, social performance staff must be "embedded" within local mine management. As the Rio Tinto board review notes: "structural arrangements are important facilitators of organisational connectedness".[26] The reference to embedding is precisely what the dual reporting lines for the tailings facility engineer in Figure 8.1 is intended to achieve. Indeed, if the position of the tailings facility engineer in the figure were replaced with a social performance specialist, and the role of the accountable executive expanded as recommended above, Figure 8.1 would describe very closely what Rio Tinto intends to put in place.

Companies tend to implement such organisational arrangements after a disaster that affects the whole corporation. The Juukan Gorge matter was, among other things, a corporate public relations disaster. It was treated as such — 3 senior executives lost their jobs. Further details of how they came to lose their jobs are provided in Chapter 12.

The Standard

An early draft of the Standard specified that there should be executive managers for social and environmental performance.[27] However, this proposal was eliminated

---

[24] Owen, J and Kemp, D, op cit, Chapter 12.

[25] Rio Tinto, "Board Review of Cultural Heritage Management" 23 August 2020. The Juukan Gorge incident is discussed earlier in this book (see Chapter 6).

[26] Ibid p 67.

[27] Version of 26 August 2019, requirement 4.a.4. "The Board of Directors of corporations involved in mining shall designate an executive manager for safety and operational risk, an executive manager for social performance and an executive manager for environmental performance. The executive manager for safety and operational risk should normally be the executive accountable for TSF safety".

quite early in the process because this was judged to be beyond the scope of the Standard, which was to prevent catastrophic tailings facility failure. What remains of the proposal in the final Standard is the requirement that the accountable executive:

> "... shall be accountable for the safety of tailings facilities and for avoiding or minimising the social and environmental consequences of a tailings facility failure".

The example in Box 8.3 does not involve a tailings facility failure and so is not covered by the Standard. It does, however, highlight the need for the more general approach to the protection of local communities from harm that we have sketched in this chapter. Let us suppose that Rio Tinto had social performance staff in its Iron Ore business unit who worked onsite and who reported up a separate functional line to a social performance manager on the corporate executive who exercised authority in these matters. This would probably have saved the Juukan Gorge caves from destruction.

Conclusion

Business corporations are under enormous pressure to maximise shareholder returns. This is most clearly revealed by looking at the bonus arrangements for top executives, which overwhelmingly emphasise shareholder returns. These incentive arrangements cascade downwards, bringing commercial pressure to bear throughout most of the organisation. This will most certainly undermine safety, particularly in relation to major accident risks, unless powerful countervailing forces exist within the corporation. The most effective way to achieve this for large corporations is to set up "functions" devoted to managing major accident risk effectively. These functions must be headed by an executive who sits on the top management team of the corporation, who is not responsible for any commercial activity, whose remuneration does not depend in any way on shareholder returns and who has unfettered access to the board. This executive must have sufficient staff to ensure proper risk management throughout the corporation. Companies that operate largely autonomous business units – in particular, mining companies, resist these ideas. But inquiries after major accidents frequently highlight their importance. In particular, the Northfleet report on the Brumadinho tragedy stressed the importance of these principles, as we showed in Chapter 2. We have also argued that these ideas apply to the effective management of social and environmental performance. That is the lesson that Rio Tinto drew from its Juukan Gorge disaster.

CHAPTER 9

The goal of zero fatalities

The very first sentence of the preamble to the Standard states that it:

> "... strives to achieve the ultimate goal of zero harm to people and the environment with zero tolerance for human fatality."

This is a ringing statement, especially the idea of "zero tolerance for human fatality".

It is painful for us to read these words now because the reality is that the Standard manifestly fails to show zero tolerance for human fatality. The panel struggled with this, coming back to it again and again, but it is one of the matters on which conventional technical views and realism won the day, as described in Chapter 4. In this chapter, we outline 2 main ways in which the Standard does not live up to that powerful assertion in its very first sentence. The first concerns the classification of facilities in terms of the consequences, should they fail, and the second is the idea of acceptable risk.

Classification by consequence

The terms of reference for the Global Tailings Review (GTR) asked the panel to devise:

> "A global and transparent consequence-based tailings facility classification system with appropriate requirements for each level of classification."

What was required was a system for classifying tailings facilities based on the scale of consequences to be expected should the facility suddenly collapse, regardless of how unlikely such a collapse might be. Those consequences would include the expected number of fatalities among people downstream, the extent of damage to the environment, effect on infrastructure and so on.

The panel was not in a position to develop its own classification system. It decided, therefore, to start from a draft that had been prepared by the International Commission on Large Dams (ICOLD), specifically for tailings facilities. The intention was to modify the draft to suit the panel's purposes. The question was: what were those purposes? In particular, could the ICOLD classification be modified so that it exhibited zero tolerance for human fatality? Given this purpose, we focus here only on the way fatality numbers influenced the classification of a facility, ignoring the environmental, infrastructure and other factors that might influence the classification. We do this in Table 9.1. Please bear with us. This discussion may seem laboured, but it is necessary, if we are to understand the issues.

Table 9.1 ICOLD and Zero Tolerance consequence classifications.

Column 1 ICOLD consequence classification	Column 2 ICOLD criteria	Column 3 Clarified ICOLD criteria	Column 4 "Zero Tolerance" classification
	Potential loss of life	Probable loss of life	
Low	None expected	None expected	Significant
Significant	Unspecified	<1	Significant
High	Possible 1–10	1–10	Extreme
Very high	Likely 10–100	10–100	Extreme
Extreme	Many >100	>100	Extreme

The first column in Table 9.1 names the 5 consequence categories in the ICOLD table – low to extreme. The next column represents the criteria that correspond to these categories. At this point, unfortunately, things become confusing. The first problem is the meaning of *potential* loss of life. Does this mean possible or probable? It is always *possible* that even with no inhabitants downstream, someone might be walking in the area at the time the dam fails and be killed by the flow of tailings. So, if potential means possible, then potential loss of life is always at least one. On the other hand, if potential means probable, and the area downstream of the dam is uninhabited, then it is unlikely (improbable) that anyone will be in the area at the particular time of failure, in which case the potential loss of life is zero. In the dam classification context, potential loss of life usually means probable loss of life, so in column 3, which is an attempt to clarify the intention of the ICOLD formulation, we use the term probable loss of life.

Consider now the categories "high", "very high" and "extreme". In column 2, these are given conflicting meanings. The most sensible are the numerical equivalents 1–10, 10–100 and >100. However, these are equated with "possible", "likely" and "many". This raises the questions: *what* is possible and *what* is likely? There are no clear answers to these questions, so these descriptive words mean nothing in this context. Hence, they are omitted in column 3.

The second category of failure is "significant". The loss of life in this case is "unspecified" in column 2. That is clearly unsatisfactory for a system of classification. Given that we have clarified that "high" means 1–10, "significant" must mean less than one, as indicated in column 3. In this context, a number less than one must be interpreted as a probability of the loss of one life.[1] This corresponds to a situation with no permanent population downstream, but a small number of people temporarily in the area from time to time, for example, hunters or herders. Where there is not even a temporary presence of this nature, the classification is "low", and it is reasonable to say that no loss of life is expected.

The clarified ICOLD version enables us to see more clearly what the ICOLD classification implies. In the first 2 categories (low and significant), the probability that any life is lost is less than one, possibly a lot less than one if people are present only occasionally. For the categories "high", "very high" and "extreme", at least one fatality is likely to occur, if the dam fails. (We come to column 4 in a moment.)

---

[1] damsafety.nsw.gov.au/wp-content/uploads/DSC3A.pdf, p 11.

There are several uses of a consequence classification like this. One is to determine the standard to which the dam will be built. The ICOLD guidance requires that the standard of construction should be increased progressively from low to extreme. This means, in particular, that a dam that has a consequence classification of "high", 1–10 expected fatalities, is built to a lower standard than a dam that could kill 10–100 or >100 if it failed. Logically, this implies a greater tolerance of a small number of fatalities than a larger number of fatalities. On the face of it, it is inconsistent with the stated objective of zero tolerance for human fatality.

This problem was noted in various public submissions and the expert panel struggled with it at length. The implication was that the panel needed to classify as extreme any dam whose failure would probably lead to at least one fatality. This alternative "zero tolerance" scheme is presented in the last column of the table.

There is ample precedent for this alternative scheme. There are many systems of consequence classification that group into a single extreme consequence category all dams whose failure would probably lead to at least one fatality.[2]

However, opinion was divided within the expert panel on the desirability of grouping the 3 highest consequence categories together in this way. It was suggested that design engineers would inevitably distinguish between high, very high and extreme consequence dams and that the higher the consequence level, the more stringent the design criteria they would use, regardless of the classification the panel adopted. (We explain why the tailings engineers would think this way in the next section.) Moreover, the technical subgroup of the International Council for Mining and Metals (ICMM), mentioned in Chapter 4, was urging the adoption of the ICOLD draft, unmodified. In the end, the panel bowed to "realism" and accepted the ICOLD draft, with all its defects. In so doing, it lost an opportunity to give expression to the goal of zero tolerance for human fatality.

It is possible to argue that this failure is not as bad as it appears. When mining is finished and tailings facilities are to be signed off as safe in perpetuity, the Standard requires that they be finished off to the highest standard (extreme), regardless of their initial consequence classification.[3] Moreover, requirement 4.2 requires designers to demonstrate that whatever initial design standard is chosen, it will still be possible to finish off the facility to the highest standard. Companies should quickly realise that there is little to be saved by constructing tailings facilities to lower standards at the beginning of their life cycle, when at the end of the cycle they will have to be upgraded to the highest standard.

Requirement 4.2 went through many iterations and was intended as a non-confrontational way to ensure that all facilities would be built to the highest standard. However, it allows companies to put off expenditure to a date that is possibly many decades away, something that is always attractive to them, particularly if the mine is not yet in operation or generating an income stream. Moreover, there remains the risk that if a mine with its associated tailings facility is sold before the end of the life cycle

[2] For example, Federal Emergency Management Agency (FEMA), *Selecting and Accommodating Inflow Design Floods for Dams*, US 2013, FEMA P-94, p 10. fema.gov/media-library-data/1386108128706-02191a433d6a703f8dbdd68cde574a0a/Selecting_and_Accommodating_Inflow_Design_Floods_for_Dams.PDF See also Email responses, op cit, Earthworks.
[3] See tables 2 and 3 in Annex 2 of the Standard.

to a company that is not a signatory to the Standard, the facility may never be closed to the highest standard.

It remains the case, however, that by adopting the ICOLD consequence classification, the panel lost an opportunity to give expression to the goal of zero tolerance for human fatality.

Acceptable risk

We noted above that tailings facility engineers will want to build to a standard that is determined by the number of deaths that might be expected in the event of failure: the higher the number of deaths, the more stringent will be the design criteria. This is the outcome of a particular way of thinking, namely that risk can never be entirely eliminated and that the best that can be done is to adopt design criteria that reduce the likelihood of failure to such a low level that the risk can be said to be acceptable. This is an ingrained way of thinking in many walks of life and it would be unrealistic to expect our Standard to be able to overturn it in the case of tailings dams.

Nevertheless, in our view it is a flawed way of thinking. Our aim here is to expose some of the flaws and propose an alternative way of thinking about risk that would justify the zero-tolerance approach described above. Our focus is specifically on individual fatality risk.

To begin with, we might ask who judges a fatality risk to be acceptable. If a risk is voluntarily assumed, for example the risk of being killed while rock-climbing, then it is the climber who implicitly judges the risk to be acceptable.[4] However, many, if not most, risks are *imposed* to varying degrees on those who may suffer the consequences. Where a tailings dam is constructed upstream from an existing settlement, and residents have no opportunity to participate in siting or design decisions, and no power of veto, then this is clearly an imposed risk. The risk may be quite unacceptable to many of these residents.

Risk analysts do not normally consider whether the risk is acceptable to those on whom the risk is imposed. Rather the question is whether the risk is acceptable to "society". This does not make much sense. Society is not in a position to accept risk; governments might, on behalf of society, but society is not an entity that can make these normative judgements. So what do risk analysts mean when they talk about acceptable risk? For those who are not imbued with the conventional risk analytic perspective, the answer is truly extraordinary, as we hope to show in what follows.

In a nutshell, the analyst takes 2 steps. The first step is to establish the existing fatality risk for people in the situation of concern. The second step is to declare this to be acceptable. There are important qualifications to this blunt statement, some of which we deal with shortly, but this, broadly speaking, is the situation. For instance, if the actual fatality rate among industrial workers is one death per 1,000 per year, then this must mean that society has *accepted* it. And if society has accepted it,

---

4   Health and Safety Executive (HSE), *Reducing Risks, Protecting People, HSE's Decision Making Process*, HMSO, Norwich 2001. See also Owen, J, and Kemp, D, Displaced by mine waste: The social consequences of industrial risk-taking, *The Extractive Industries and Society* 2019, 6: pp 424–427.

this means that society has judged it to be *acceptable*. In this way, the current risk level becomes the acceptable risk level. A statement of what is the case becomes a statement of what ought to be the case. A factual statement is transformed into a normative one.

Here is a real example that demonstrates the point. Some years ago, the United Kingdom's Railtrack Corporation laid out the tolerable levels of risk for different categories of stakeholders.[5] For rail track workers, it was one death per 1,000 per year, while for rail passengers it was one in 10,000 per year.[6] Why the difference?

One justification that is sometimes provided for such differences is the degree to which the risks are voluntarily assumed – the greater the degree of choice involved, the higher the acceptable level of risk. Could this be the explanation? Is it the case that rail workers voluntarily accept the risk by going to work, while rail travellers, most of whom are commuters, do not? The fact is that commuters take steps daily to put themselves at risk by boarding trains to go to work. In this way they are no different from rail employees who daily put themselves at risk by being at work. The point is that *going* to work is no more voluntary or involuntary than *being* at work. If that is agreed, then the different circumstances of rail workers and commuters provides no justification for arguing that the acceptable level of risk for rail employees is 10 times higher than it is for rail commuters. So how were these figures arrived at? The answer is they are derived from the *existing* fatality rates of these 2 groups. The implicit assumption was that because rail employees were killed at 10 times the rate of passengers, this must be acceptable. Used in this way, the idea of acceptable risk simply serves to legitimise the status quo.

However, we believe that rather than seeing the existing distribution of risk as a result of some kind of value consensus, it is better to see it as the outcome of a political process, the result of a contest between unequal political forces. Rail track workers would clearly like to have a workplace that was 10 times safer, but they are not a politically influential group, and given existing resources and rail track priorities, this is quite beyond their reach. For example, one way to protect the lives of track workers more effectively is to give them "possession" of the track on which they are working. This would mean excluding or diverting trains. Such a solution would be contrary to the interests of commuters, so workers are not given track possession, as a matter of course, and must rely in part on lookouts to warn them of approaching trains.

In contrast, the political influence of commuters results in the provision of expensive infrastructure to enhance passenger safety, such as signalling systems and automatic train stops. Every major rail crash results in a public inquiry that creates further pressure for safety improvements.

To repeat, existing fatality rates are best seen as a result of these various political processes. They should not be seen as the result of some society-wide value consensus.

It is at this point that we must introduce an important qualification. These limits of acceptability tend to be set on an industry or society-wide basis. They then

---

[5] We are using the words tolerable and acceptable interchangeably here. In some contexts, a distinction is made, but this makes no difference to our argument.
[6] Hopkins, A, *Safety, Culture and Risk*, Sydney: CCH 2005, pp 123–124

become benchmarks against which subgroups can be assessed. So, if passengers travelling on trains belonging to a particular company have a fatality risk that is twice the industry figure, it is unlikely that the authorities would treat this as an acceptable risk for this particular company. In this context, the industry-wide risk level becomes a standard to which poor-performing companies may be held. Used in this way, acceptable risk is no longer a justification or the status quo but becomes potentially a means of driving safety improvements.

Sometimes inter-industry comparisons can also be used in this way to argue for higher safety standards and, surprisingly, against them. One argument made to the expert panel involved a comparison of the ability of *buildings* to withstand earthquakes with the corresponding ability of *tailings facilities*. The relevance is that a building that collapses in an earthquake can kill many people, just as can extreme consequence tailings facilities. The argument was that to construct all tailings facilities to the standard required for extreme consequence facilities would make lower consequence dams safer than buildings, with respect to earthquake risk.[7] From a society-wide viewpoint, this was unreasonable. Hence, so the argument went, it was important to use a graduated set of design criteria to correspond to a graduated set of consequences. This would ensure that fatality risks for some tailings dams did not end up substantially lower than in other human arenas.

This discussion leads to an important conclusion. We have argued that so-called acceptable levels of risk are essentially the outcome of political processes, not of any society-wide consensus. If that is the case, there is no reason why risk levels associated with tailings facilities should *not* be lower than in other risk arenas. The creation of the Standard occurred at a particular juncture at which the legitimacy of the industry was in question. This provided the creators of the Standard with a political opportunity to drive risks lower by requiring that all dams where failure could be expected to cause even one fatality should be built to the highest standard. Our vision here is of risk standards in different arenas leapfrogging each other to higher levels, as political circumstances allow, rather than moving towards a common level that is based in some way on what is currently the case. If the expert panel had understood all this clearly at the time, it might have pushed harder for the zero tolerance of human fatalities to which the Standard aspires.

The Mount Polley Report

The failure to follow through on the Standard's announced zero tolerance of human fatality is particularly disturbing in view of the report on the Mount Polley tailings facility failure. This was a Canadian facility that failed in 2014, killing no one, but doing major environmental damage. Canada has been at the forefront in the prevention of tailings facility failures, and the fact that Canada, of all countries, could suffer such a failure was a shock to many in the industry. Accordingly, 2 major reports were written on the failure, one by the regulator and one by an independent expert panel.

---

[7]   Australian Standard (AS) 1170.4-2007, *Structural design actions – Part 4: Earthquake actions in Australia.* saiglobal.com/PDFTemp/Previews/OSH/AS/AS1000/1100/1170.4-2007.pdf.

The independent expert panel consisted of 3 geotechnical engineers at the pinnacle of their profession. Their report championed the idea of zero tolerance of fatality risk, far more effectively than does the Standard. Here are its words:

> "In risk-based dam safety practice for conventional water dams, some particular level of tolerable risk is often specified that, in turn, implies some tolerable failure rate. The panel does not accept the concept of a tolerable failure rate for tailings dams. To do so, no matter how small, would institutionalize failure. First Nations will not accept this, the public will not permit it, government will not allow it, and the mining industry will not survive it."

One of the Mount Polley panel members reiterated the point in a later publication:

> "[the panel] recommended that the industry establish a path to zero failure, as opposed to some tolerable failure rate".[8]

This contradicts the whole idea of acceptable risk.

Another remarkable statement made by the Mount Polley panel was the following:

> "Safety attributes should be evaluated separately from economic considerations, and cost should not be the determining factor."[9]

This is a direct challenge to a ubiquitous philosophy of ALARP, which requires that risks be reduced to *as low as reasonably practicable*. The concept of ALARP is used throughout the Standard. It is defined in the glossary as follows:

> "ALARP requires that all reasonable measures be taken with respect to 'tolerable' or acceptable risks to reduce them even further until the cost and other impacts of additional risk reduction are grossly disproportionate to the benefit."

This involves a weighing of costs and benefits, which is precisely what the Mount Polley panel said should not be done.[10] Of course, the Mount Polley panel recognised that there is a limit on how much can be spent on safety. Ultimately, therefore, its statement must be regarded as aspirational.

Conclusion

The position taken by the engineers who wrote the Mount Polley report is remarkable. In principle, they reject the idea of a tolerable or acceptable risk of tailings dam failure. It follows that for these engineers, there is no fatality risk level that can be deemed acceptable. Although their report was written 5 years prior to the GTR, it comes much closer to articulating the vision of zero tolerance for human fatality than the Standard does. The Standard is a retreat in this respect. We can only attribute this to the politically charged context in which it was created.

---

[8] Morgenstern, Mello Lecture, op cit, p 121.

[9] Independent Expert Engineering Investigation and Review Panel, *Report on Mount Polley Tailings Storage Facility Breach*, 30 January 2015, p 125. mountpolleyreviewpanel.ca/sites/default/files/report/ ReportonMountPolleyTailingsStorageFacilityBreach.pdf.

[10] In some risk regimes the idea of gross disproportionality is given a precise meaning: if the cost of some risk reduction measure is more than ten times the monetary benefits, it is not justified. Performing this calculation requires that a monetary value be placed on lives saved.

CHAPTER 10

Consequence-based decision-making[1]

Suppose a mining company is trying to decide whether to build a tailings facility in a valley just above a population centre that would be obliterated if the facility failed. How should it make its decision? A purely risk-based approach to decision-making would argue as follows. Provided the facility is designed and operated to a high-enough standard, the probability of failure can be made so low that the risk can be regarded as acceptable.

On the other hand, one of the undoubted achievements of the Standard is its adoption of the idea that decision-making about preventing unwanted events should not be based on assessments of risk alone. It must also consider, independently, the severity of the consequence. The ultimate implication of this view is that if the consequences of a facility failure are severe enough, then no matter how low the probability, the construction of the facility cannot be justified. The aim of this chapter is to clarify this reasoning and to discuss the extent to which it was incorporated in the Standard.[2]

Risk matrices

The meaning of "risk" varies greatly with the context.[3] In what follows, the context of interest is company decision-making about unwanted events. The conventional view in this context is that risk is a 2-dimensional concept – the 2 dimensions being "likelihood" and "consequence". The higher the likelihood, the greater the risk and likewise, the higher the consequence, the greater the risk. This is represented as a risk matrix. Figure 10.1 is a typical matrix, in this case used by the Mining Association of Canada.[4]

---

[1] Thanks to Gerry Burke for his invaluable comments on an earlier draft of this chapter. Of course, he bears no responsibility for the final version.

[2] Some of the thinking/material included in this chapter was captured in explanatory notes/background papers as part of the expert panel process. However, these documents were never finalised and therefore not shared publicly.

[3] Aven, T, The risk concept – historical and recent development trends, *Reliability Engineering and System Safety*, 2012, 99: pp 33–44.
[4] The Mining Association of Canada, *A Guide to the Management of Tailings Facilities*, 3rd ed, p 41. mining.ca/wp-content/uploads/2019/03/MAC-Tailings-Guide_2019.pdf.

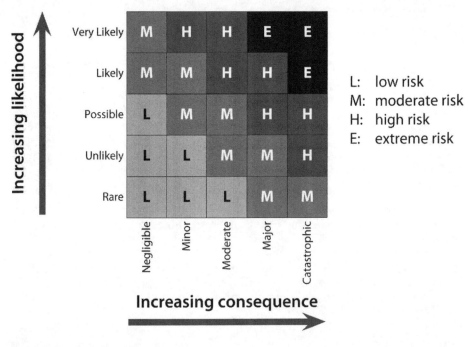

Figure 10.1 Typical risk matrix

The risk matrix in Figure 10.1 is symmetrical, so it confers equal weight to consequence and likelihood. This means that a high likelihood but low-consequence event has the same risk as a low likelihood but high-consequence event. This is problematic. It is unrealistic to equate a likely event with negligible consequences, the sort of accident that many of us will have experienced, with a catastrophic accident that happens rarely.

Many companies have a policy that the higher the risk, the higher the organisational level at which decisions about risk acceptability are made. But in Figure 10.1, catastrophic events that occur only rarely are not extreme risks and may never be considered at the highest levels of the company. The result is that executive committees and boards may have little understanding of the catastrophic possibilities to which the company is exposed and which they are implicitly endorsing.

This is one of the reasons that there is now a move to replace risk-based decision-making with consequence-based decision-making in some situations. We shall provide an example shortly.

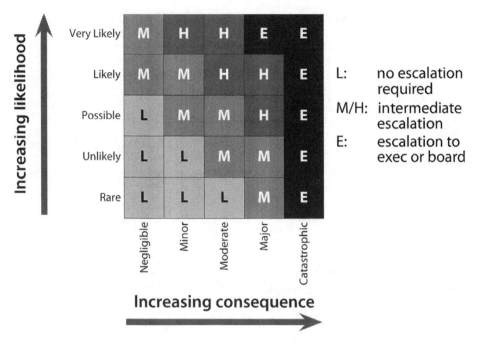

Figure 10.2 A modified risk matrix

Figure 10.2 above is a modified risk matrix that represents this new approach. It is no longer symmetrical. It ranks all catastrophic possibilities as extreme, regardless of their associated likelihood. All such possibilities must be elevated to the executive committee or the board for consideration. Decision-makers at this level may decide that no matter how low the likelihood, they are not comfortable accepting a proposal where the consequences of failure are catastrophic. They might therefore decide that additional measures are necessary to reduce the potential consequences of failure before they are willing to endorse the proposal.[5]

This approach does not mean that "likelihood" is totally irrelevant in considering the appropriate response to rare but catastrophic events. But the question of likelihood is transformed into a more subjective question of how much one is willing to spend to reduce the consequences of failure.

Risk analysts will be uncomfortable with the idea of uncoupling likelihood from the risk in this way. This discomfort can be dealt with by eliminating the concept of "risk" from the matrix altogether and treating it as a "decision-escalation" matrix as follows: L in the matrix means no escalation of decision-making is required, E means that the matter must be escalated to the executive committee or the board for a decision, M and H mean that intermediate levels of escalation are required.

---

[5] For further discussion see Hopkins, A, How Much Should be Spent to Prevent Disaster? A Critique of Consequence Times Probability, *The Journal of Pipeline Engineering*, 2015, 2nd Q.

There is a second reason why it is important to focus on consequences rather than risk when dealing with catastrophic events. Dam designers will argue that it is possible to design facilities with such a low probability of failure that the risk (probability × consequence) is acceptable, even though, in the extremely unlikely event of failure, the consequence would be catastrophic. Designers typically assume that the facility will be built and operated in accordance with their design intent. Herein lies the problem. Tailings dams are constructed over decades with the dam wall being raised from time to time as the volume of tailings grows. If economic circumstances change, or if ownership changes, there is no guarantee that the facility will be built and maintained as the designers intended.[6]

According to one expert, the "vast majority of dam failures have occurred [because of] … 'chains' of gradual deviances, which become 'normalized' over time"[7], resulting in poor construction, maintenance or management. In short, the real probability of failure of these dams was much higher than the design assumed. The problem is that this real probability is unknowable beforehand.

Other writers put the point even more bluntly: "Negligent and insufficient maintenance or inadequate procedures for operation are decisive factors in dam safety, but they cannot be considered by a probabilistic assessment".[8]

In light of this, the only sure way to make dams safer is to focus on driving down the consequences of failure no matter how low the presumed probability may be. In the context of tailings dams, the additional consequence-reduction measures might include diversionary dams, barriers and other engineering solutions below the tailings facility. For new facilities, it may be possible to position the facility on the site in such a way that these additional works can be constructed within the site boundary. This option may not be available for existing facilities, in which case it will be necessary to liaise with or secure approval from other parties, such as government agencies, local municipalities and other landowners and users. Another possibility is to negotiate to resettle populations at risk in the valley below. Designers will typically not consider these offsite solutions, but the ultimate decision-makers can and should.

A precedent for consequence-based decision-making

There are precedents for consequence-based decision-making in other industries. In 2005, BP experienced an explosion at the Texas City Refinery at one of its petroleum processing units. Fifteen workers were killed. They were doing maintenance work

---

[6] Herza, J and Phillips, J, *Design of dams for mining industry*, 85th Annual Meeting of the International Commission on Large Dams, Prague, Czech Republic, 3–7 July 2017, section 11.5.

[7] Oboni, F, Oboni, C and Brehaut, H, *Tailings Dam Management for the Twenty-First Century*, Springer International Publishing, Kindle Edition, Location 1387.

[8] Herza, J, Ashley, M, Thorp, J and Small, A, *A consequence-based tailings dam safety framework*, Symposium of the International Commission on Large Dams (ICOLD), Ottawa, Canada, 9–14 June 2019.

during a shutdown and were housed in flimsy temporary buildings close to the process unit. The location of the temporary buildings had been risk-assessed and the risks judged to be as low as reasonably practicable. But the risk assessment was grossly inadequate. After the disaster, BP decided that, henceforth, the location of all buildings that were not explosion-proof would depend on the potential consequences of process unit explosions, regardless of the likelihood of such an event. Buildings would need to be sited beyond the range of any possible explosion.[9]

This lesson was widely disseminated and at least one mining company engaged in minerals processing decided at board level that it would need to relocate many of its office buildings that were too close to explosion sources. The additional feature of this case is that one of the business units concerned could not afford the expense and the board made the decision that the relocation would be funded from the corporate centre.

We note that most of the people who died in the Brumadinho disaster were workers located in buildings immediately below the dam wall. Had the siting of these buildings been subject to a consequence assessment, they could never have been located where they were.

The Standard

Focussing now on the Standard, it implements both ideas discussed above: first, that the higher the consequence, the higher the organisational level at which approval must be given, and second, that safety is best served by focussing on consequence reduction, in addition to the reduction of risk.

Requirement 5.7 specifies that for proposed new dams, where the hypothetical failure of the dam would cause one or more fatalities, construction approval must be given by a senior executive of the company – the accountable executive. Moreover, this approver is required to consider whether any additional reasonable steps beyond those envisaged by the designers can be taken downstream, to reduce potential consequences. For existing facilities, at every 5-yearly review, the same senior executive must "seek to identify and implement additional reasonable steps that may be taken to further reduce potential consequences to people and the environment". The focus in this requirement, consequence reduction, independently of risk reduction, is a step change beyond current practice.

Consequence-reducing possibilities that the panel had in mind would be to build levees around downstream population centres, build emergency barriers to catch tailings flows or use multiple smaller dams that could not fail simultaneously. These ideas were included in an early draft of the Standard. However, they met with some resistance and were ultimately edited out. The Standard has been criticised, rightly in our view, for having failed to mention such possibilities explicitly.

---

[9]   Hopkins A, *Failure to Learn: The BP Texas City Refinery Disaster*, CCH, Sydney, 2008.

Intolerable consequences

We noted at the outset of this chapter that one potential implication of the consequence-based approach is that if the consequences of a facility failure are severe enough, then no matter how low the probability, the construction of the facility cannot be justified. Putting it another way, in this situation it is not just the risk (probability × consequence) that is intolerable but the consequences themselves. Note here that we are using the words "intolerable" and "unacceptable" interchangeably.

The expert panel initially considered adopting this idea. The suggestion was that companies should specify an upper limit to the level of consequence (say the number of fatalities) that would be regarded as tolerable. They would then need to commit to abandoning any construction proposal that breached that limit, or at least modifying it to reduce the consequences of failure to a tolerable level.

This suggestion met with stiff resistance from various quarters, in particular, from the technical working group set up by the International Council for Mining and Metals (ICMM). The argument was that an aircraft crash can kill hundreds, while a nuclear power station accident could kill thousands. If those consequences are not regarded as intolerable, why should tailings dams be subjected to absolute limits on potential consequences? This argument was not put to the panel in writing; it was relayed indirectly. But the panel were forced to conclude that this was one of the ICMM's non-negotiables. Reluctantly, the panel bowed to "realism" (see discussion in Chapter 4) and abandoned the idea.

The fact is, however, that specifying a limit to the consequences that will be tolerable is well accepted in some contexts and has influential supporters even among tailings facility engineers. In particular, one of the most revered of these engineers, Norbert Morgenstern, raises the matter in his widely read de Mello lecture of 2018.[10] The topic is technical and we hesitated before deciding to canvas it here, but we believe it is important that the reader consider these ideas.

Morgenstern bases his analysis on the fatalities from landslides in Hong Kong. See figure 10.3 below. This figure is taken from Morgenstern's de Mello lecture but contains more information than is needed for present purposes. What is important here is that everything above and to the right of the heavy black line is intolerable (unacceptable), while everything below and to the left is tolerable, in varying degrees.

---

[10] Morgenstern, N, Geotechnical Risk, Regulation, and Public Policy (Victor de Mello Lecture), *Soils and Rocks*, May–August, 2018, 41(2): pp 107–129.

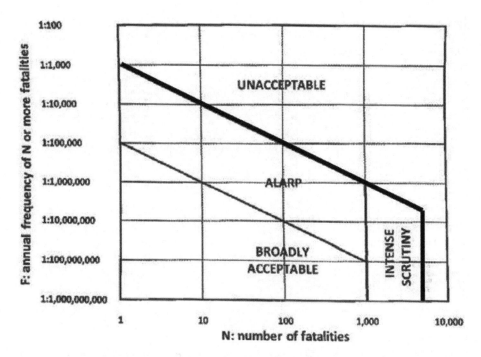

Figure 10.3 Limits of acceptability for Hong Kong landslide risk

Here is a little more detail on how to interpret the diagram. The vertical axis is the probability of a landslide that kills a specified number of people. That probability ranges from once in 100 years to once in 1,000,000,000 years. The horizontal axis is the number of people killed, ranging from one to 10,000. So, consider a landslide that kills 10 people. This is judged to be an intolerable (unacceptable) risk if it occurs more often than once in 10,000 years.

The line defining intolerable (unacceptable) risk runs downwards to a probability of about one in 4,000,000 years, corresponding with an event causing roughly 4,000 fatalities. (The numbers are difficult to read off the graph because the axes are logarithmic, not linear.) At this point the line turns vertically downwards. This represents an absolute limit on the tolerability of numbers killed. If more than 4,000 people could be killed, then no matter how low the probability, that is how low the risk, the *consequence* is intolerable, and something must be done. In the Hong Kong case, that meant the government needed to legislate to reduce the number of people exposed.

The precise turning point of this tolerability curve, that is the number of fatalities that will be regarded as intolerable, regardless of probability, is not something that can be determined in any objective way. If the decision is being made by government, as in the Hong Kong case, the matter requires extensive consultation to determine the extent of public willingness to accept some level of risk for the sake of affordable residential land or other trade-offs.

Furthermore, probabilities of failure below about one in a million cannot be realistically determined. They are beyond the limits of risk analysis and have been described as "not credible", or even as "acts of God".[11] This is another reason it makes sense to truncate the tolerability line in the vicinity of one in a million, as in the Hong Kong case.[12]

According to Morgenstern, the Hong Kong limit of tolerability "made sense" when he translated it into the context of tailings dam failures in Canada. (He does not expand on what "made sense" means.) However, as he also makes clear, this approach to determining the limit of tolerability is only possible where civil society is sufficiently organised and educated to be able to express views about the trade-offs that may be involved, and governments are willing to act on this basis.

All this provides further support for the idea that, for tailings facility failures, it is appropriate to regard some level of consequence as intolerable, regardless of probability. It does not however provide support for any specific limit.

The expert panel was not originally proposing that a specific number of fatalities should be specified in the Standard as intolerable merely that, as a first step, companies should specify their own limits and make these known. Such a requirement would have enshrined in the Standard the idea that some consequences are so severe that they cannot be contemplated.

So, to return to the question with which we started this section, on the Morgenstern numbers, if the population immediately below the proposed dam was more than 4,000, the dam could not be built. We suspect that many companies, if required to specify a limit of tolerable consequences, would choose a figure much less than 4,000.

Conclusion

We concluded in the previous chapter that the Standard fell well short of its proclaimed goal of "zero tolerance for human fatality". Arguably such a goal can never be more than aspirational. On the other hand, this chapter argues that it is realistic to have zero tolerance for some specific number of fatalities. Unfortunately, the Standard proposes no such limitation. This was another opportunity missed.

---

[11] Oboni, F, Oboni, C and Brehaut, H, op cit, Location 2423.
[12] As noted earlier, in the Hong Kong case the figure appears to be about 1 in 4 million.

CHAPTER 11

Implementation of the Standard

The Standard contains many step changes. Requirements for human rights due diligence, clear internal accountabilities and increased public disclosure are amongst the centrepieces. However, the point of the Global Tailings Review (GTR) was not to produce a document, but to influence practice on the ground. The vital question that this chapter addresses, then, is the question of implementation. This includes more than the operationalisation of the Standard by companies. It also includes oversight and governance of the Standard itself. Without independent oversight, the International Council for Mining and Metals (ICMM) may as well have developed its own standard for its members to apply as they please. This chapter outlines a range of issues associated with implementation, and the extent to which future plans are likely to restore the confidence of investors and host communities.

The implementation vision at the time of launch

ICMM members agreed to implement the Standard even before the expert panel put pen to paper. The United Nations Environment Program (UNEP) and the Principles for Responsible Investment (PRI) were not as specific as the ICMM in terms of committing to action before the Standard was written. The stakes were therefore higher for the ICMM than for the other co-conveners, particularly if the industry was to survive its "crisis of credibility".

At the launch of the Standard in August 2020, all 3 organisations emphasised the importance of implementation.[1] The ICMM reconfirmed that its members would move to immediate implementation. According to its CEO:

> "The Standard will be integrated into ICMM's existing member commitments, which includes third party assurance and validation, and we are in the process of developing supporting guidance. Members have committed that all facilities with 'extreme' or 'very high' potential consequences will be in conformance with the Standard within three years of today, and all other facilities within five years."

In responses to questions posed to the presenters at the launch event, the ICMM confirmed that its members were willing to participate in discussions about the establishment of an independent entity, but that the ICMM would not take the lead.

UNEP's launch statements noted that the Standard's impact would depend upon uptake, and expressed support of an independent entity. UNEP stated:

> "In order to maintain the integrity of the Standard, it is crucial that a non-industry organisation identify and pursue the most effective implementation model such as the establishment of an independent entity. To this end, UNEP will continue to engage in dialogue with other interested stakeholders to explore potential solutions."

---

[1] See launch statements by UNEP, the PRI and the ICMM. globaltailingsreview.org/new-global-industry-standard-on-tailings-management-aims-to-improve-the-safety-of-tailings-facilities-in-the-mining-industry/.

The PRI's representative organisations, the Church of England Pensions Board and the Council on Ethics for the Swedish National Pension Funds, emphasised 2 points about the pathway to implementation. Speaking to uptake by industry, the Swedish funds noted:

"We expect all mining companies to comply with this framework, and responsible investors looking to address the risks of tailings failure now have a responsibility to drive implementation, incorporating the Standard into stewardship and active ownership strategies."

Speaking to the question of oversight, the Church of England Pensions Board stated:

"For the first time we have a global Standard that goes beyond existing best practice and establishes the most comprehensive Standard that Investors will hold companies accountable for in their implementation. I look forward to working with all parties to establish an independent entity which will oversee the implementation of the Standard."

In their various public appearances following the launch, the co-convening organisations have positioned the Standard as a "first step" towards safe tailings management, emphasising that there is much work to do to implement the Standard.

Pathways to implementation

At the time of the launch, the independent chair of the GTR hoped that the Standard would have a home separate to, but supported by, the mining industry. He said:

"It has been a privilege to lead this work and I now call on all mining companies, governments and investors to use the Standard and to continue to work together to improve the safety of tailings facilities globally. It is my hope that the Standard will be supported by an independent body that can maintain the quality and further refine and strengthen the Standard over time."

While the GTR chair did not have a mandate to establish such an entity, he nonetheless presented recommendations to the co-conveners on the matter. These recommendations appear in the final chapter of the GTR Compendium of Papers.[2] The chair and his co-authors argue that:

"Without an effective implementation strategy, the time, effort and resources invested in building the Standard could dissipate and the problems which give rise to the GTR persist. Involving all three co-conveners will also help to ensure that the Standard continues to be viewed as a multi-stakeholder initiative that represents a broad range of interests."

The chapter describes a number of pathways for the roll-out of the Standard and support for its evolution, none of which are mutually exclusive. These pathways include:

- voluntary implementation by individual companies, following the new global benchmark

---

[2] Oberle, B, Bateman, P, and Kemp, D, Establishing an Independent Entity, *GTR Compendium,* Chapter XIX. globaltailingsreview.org/wp-content/uploads/2020/09/Ch-XXIX-Pathways-to-Implementation_ Establishing-an-Independent-Entity.pdf.

- industry organisations require adoption by their membership

- state-based regulation, whereby states promote the Standard through legislation, regulation, guidelines or other regulatory mechanism (eg approval conditions)

- third-party regulation, whereby banks, insurers and investment funds make compliance with the Standard conditional for accessing their products or services

- an independent entity that is not controlled by any single sector, to host the Standard, test conformance and report assessment outcomes in the public domain.

The chair emphasised that the last of these was very much the preferred option. He outlined the advantages of an independent entity as providing:

- a mechanism for institutionalising the Standard and maintaining momentum for change

- autonomy from industry and reducing the risk of "industry capture"

- a neutral space in which industry and third parties could share views about the operation and effectiveness of the Standard

- a forum for different stakeholder groups to focus on the common goal of preventing catastrophic tailings facility failures.

We make 2 additional observations about the advantages of the independent entity pathway. First, affected communities would be formally represented and given a voice, which they would otherwise not have. We say more about this shortly.

Second, one of the most important advantages, from our point of view, concerns the integrity of the assurance processes. Many of the requirements in the Standard are stated in very general terms. They need to be translated into precise terms that can be audited or assessed. This will be the job of the independent entity. This step was always envisaged with the preface to the Standard stating:

> "The Standard will be supported by implementation protocols which will provide detailed guidance for certification, or assurance as applicable, and for equivalence with other Standards."

The pathway that the ICMM is following is to draw up its own internal guidance as to how the requirements of the Standard are to be interpreted. This is no longer a tripartite process. External assurers will be hired to audit the Standard with reference to the ICMM's guidance. The risk is that this process deviates from the intent of the requirements and makes it easier for companies to achieve conformance.

Moreover, the ICMM's guidance to its member companies is just that, guidance, for companies to interpret as they wish.[3] Individual companies may modify the ICMM guidance to suit their purposes. In any particular assurance process, therefore, assurance firms may be working with documents that are twice removed from the original Standard. This would be contrary to the entire spirit of the GTR.

---

[3] See fine print at the end of the ICMM document, Assurance and Validation Procedure. icmm.com/mining-principles/assurance-and-validation/procedure.

Unfortunately, the 3 co-conveners failed to agree on the establishment of an independent entity. In the weeks and months following the launch, UNEP and the PRI have continued to advocate an independent entity, but the ICMM distanced itself from this approach. In a memo to fellow members of the ICMM's Council of CEOs, the incoming chair of the council made the following statement:

> "While making no commitments, ICMM has agreed to engage in good faith dialogue with the co-conveners on the issue of global implementation of the Standard after completion of ICMM's guidance. Many of us have reservations about the implementation/ compliance proposals by the co-conveners and other third parties. This future dialogue will be complicated, requiring thoughtful participation by ICMM."[4]

It is clear that the ICMM's preferred strategy for implementation is to go it alone. This amounts to the privatisation of the regulatory process. The risk for the ICMM is that this will undermine the credibility of any claims that its member companies make to be in conformance with the Standard.

By the time any independent entity is established, the mining industry's process for certifying itself will be established. This raises the question of why companies would then voluntarily submit to a certification process developed by the independent entity. We would not expect them to do so unless investors made it a pre-condition for investment that companies be so certified, as the PRI advocates, or if governments incorporated the Standard into their regulatory frameworks, as UNEP advocates.

However, at the time of writing, we are not optimistic that an independent entity will be established any time soon. Neither UNEP nor the PRI has made any concrete proposals, and nor is it clear where funding for the new entity will come from. We can only hope that progress will be made.

Uptake and implementation of the Standard

Although there is currently no independent entity that can systematically track industry uptake of the Standard, there is evidence that this is occurring. For instance, the ICMM reports that many of its members have established internal working groups to conduct the required self-assessments against the Standard, and address gaps in conformance.

Beyond the ICMM, other industry and certification bodies report that they are reviewing their standards to incorporate or cross-reference the new Standard, and hosting presentations, webinars and forums to discuss the Standard and encourage uptake.

State regulators have begun to reference the Standard. For instance, in a statutory review of the *Work Health and Safety (Mines and Petroleum Sites) Act 2013* and the Work Health and Safety (Mines and Petroleum Sites) Regulation 2014 in the Australian state of New South Wales, the independent reviewer recommended that:

---

4 Memo from Richard Adkerson, 9 September 2020.

"The resources regulator should reference the August 2020 Global Industry Standard on Tailings Management in its guidance material and consider potential legislative amendments to incorporate aspects of the Standard."[5]

The co-conveners have participated in a range of international forums, including those hosted by the London Metals Exchange, the World Economic Forum, the Intergovernmental Forum, the IFC Sustainability Exchange and a *Financial Times* event on the future of mining. At the *Financial Times* event in October 2020, a lawyer from international law firm White & Case indicated that the Standard was already influencing access to loan finance. Sophisticated lenders knew that it was unrealistic to demand immediate compliance and were instead requesting that mining companies identify pathways to implementation as a loan condition. Less sophisticated lenders were being blunter and asking for full and immediate compliance, which was being met with stiff resistance from borrowers. This engagement by lenders is a promising development, but questions remain as to how compliance will be assured. Without an independent entity to oversee the assurance process, lenders may not be as protected as they imagine.

We expect awareness-raising activities to continue. These events signal to the market that the industry is attuned. However, they do not build the implementation pathway envisaged at the outset of the GTR process.

The side-lining of civil society

Alongside uptake of the Standard, there was also opposition. In June 2020, an alliance of almost 150 civil society groups released an alternative set of guidelines called "Safety First: Guidelines for Responsible Mine Tailings Management".[6] This guidance calls for a more comprehensive release of information than is required in the Standard, including the public disclosure of full reports and studies, and associated raw data. As far as we know, there has been no formal response by the co-conveners, or engagement with the groups that produced this guidance, largely because the GTR was dissolved directly after the Standard was launched. Civil society groups were a vital part of the consultation processes that occurred during the development of the Standard. It would appear that they are now to be side-lined. This section outlines our concerns about this outcome.

Our first concern relates to the void created by the dissolution of the GTR and the absence of a co-ordinated response by the co-conveners to the question of the independent entity. The GTR was dissolved with no one to clarify the intent of requirements, leaving industry and its agents free to interpret the wording according to their preferences. Given the degree of industry push-back on certain requirements, it is possible that the performance bar will be lowered as implementation proceeds,

---

[5] Bills, K, Statutory Review of the NSW *Work Health and Safety (Mines and Petroleum Sites) Act 2013* and Regulation, October 2020, NSW Government. resourcesandgeoscience.nsw.gov.au/regulation/about-us/have-your-say/work-health-safety-mines-and-petroleum-sites-act-and-regulation-review.

[6] Earthworks and Mining Watch Canada, *Safety First: Guidelines for Responsible Mine Tailings Management*, June 2020. earthworks.org/publications/safety-first-guidelines-for-responsible-mine-tailings-management/.

rather than maintained or even lifted over time. Civil society will have no voice within this process. Its only option is to advocate from the side-lines.

Likewise, there is no one to monitor, track or document exactly how the industry is interpreting the requirements of the Standard, and the extent to which the original intent is being maintained. While companies have been in touch with different members of the expert panel to clarify wording, no one person holds authority to speak on behalf of the GTR. There is also the issue of consistency as the GTR network dissipates, and the collective thinking amongst the panel is lost.

We are also concerned that the GTR initiative is better servicing investors than communities at risk. While it is encouraging that the co-conveners are appearing at major international forums to promote take-up by industry, there is no parallel approach to engaging communities, or responding to queries from the grass roots. The power disparity that provided the industry with an advantage in the GTR process looks likely to continue. In other words, investors with queries are being assured that their investments are not at risk from tailings facility failures, but communities are not necessarily being assured of their safety.

This situation is a retreat from the multi-stakeholder process that underpinned the development of the Standard, and a reversion to the industry's preferred model of private regulation. This reversion runs counter to the statements made at the outset of the process, that to be credible, the GTR needed to be multi-stakeholder. ICMM members are in no way committed to the establishment of an independent entity that might constrain their interests by giving greater weight to the rights and interests of project-affected people.

The Standard involves an interdisciplinary approach to tailings management, through the integration of disciplines of social and environmental performance, and geotechnical engineering. One likely outcome of a privatised model is that this emphasis on interdisciplinary practice will soften. It is most likely that the ICMM will release guidance that focuses on the facility risks, rather than the contexts in which tailings facilities are located. We predict that, instead of pulling the disciplines together, this guidance will push social performance to the periphery once again. We are not only concerned about a reversion to private regulation, but we are also concerned about a return to the silo approach to managing tailings facilities where social performance professionals are excluded from key decisions.

There are other challenges associated with the privatised model. The development of knowledge for the public good, for instance, becomes more limited. Without an independent entity or multi-stakeholder oversight, there will be limited aggregate analysis, and limited studying of patterns across companies, commodities or other units of analysis. Likewise, there will be limited attention to issues that fall outside the scope of the Standard. For instance, the Standard did not address the issue of legacy sites. Neither did the Standard address the issue of adequate remedy for victims of tailings disasters, despite the fact that victims of the Samarco and Brumadinho disasters claim that they continue to suffer. An independent entity would be in a position to work beyond the Standard and catalyse action on these and other pressing issues.

Conclusion

The Standard was launched at a time of epic disruption. The world was in the grip of the climate change and reeling from the effects of the COVID-19 pandemic. Historic movements such as Black Lives Matter highlighted the inability of the incumbent economic and political systems to address these and other crises. The global mining industry was under pressure to maintain production and safeguard workers and communities, not only from tailings facility failures but also from the global pandemic.

In the context of such uncertainty, the future of the Standard is unclear. Nonetheless, there are several possible implementation trajectories. Ideally, an independent entity would be established to oversee implementation of the Standard, with consequences for non-conformance, to be implemented by states and/or by investors. While UNEP and the PRI have signalled their intent to establish an independent entity by the end of 2021, the current trajectory involves the industry doing what it has always done – agreeing to a performance goal, hiring private firms to assure their performance and operating without significant consequences for non-conformance.

There is a danger that after a year or 2 of implementation by mining companies, investors will be satisfied. The course is set, and if there are no disasters in the meantime, the industry may be seen to have "proved" itself. We hope this is not the case, and that UNEP and the PRI continue to push for an independent entity, with a multi-stakeholder governance structure that provides workers and affected communities with influence and a voice in the decision-making process.

As shown in detail in Chapter 2, the most important lesson to emerge from the Brumadinho disaster was the need for independent processes of assurance. The independent entity envisaged here is the only certain way of achieving that goal. Brumadinho was the impetus for the creation of the Standard and it would be a tragedy if the 3 co-conveners failed to implement the primary lesson of that disaster.

CHAPTER 12

Final reflections

One of the most interesting aspects of the creation of the Standard is that the original call was made by investors, specifically the Principles for Responsible Investment (PRI), as described in Chapter 3. Admittedly, investors did not have much influence on the content of the Standard; in this matter, it was largely industry that prevailed. But there is no doubt it was an investor group that started the ball rolling with its demand for the creation of an independent Standard in January 2019, immediately after the Brumadinho disaster. Without persistent pressure from investors, it is most unlikely that the International Council for Mining and Metals (ICMM) would have committed itself to the creation of such a Standard, particularly with a pledge from its members to comply, even before the Standard had been drafted. That was evidently quite a gamble, revealing the extent to which the ICMM members felt under pressure.

In short, round 1, the decision to construct an independent Standard went to investors. Round 2, the struggle over the content of the Standard went to the mining industry, which to a large extent outmanoeuvred the other 2 co-conveners. We reflect on these 2 rounds of engagement in subsequent sections. At the time of writing, a third round, the struggle over how the Standard will be implemented has begun. We touch on this towards the end of the chapter. We conclude with some reflections on the industry's failure to learn from the Mount Polley and Brumadinho disasters, as well as lessons to be learned from the Global Tailings Review (GTR) process itself.

The influence of investors

One of the most interesting, dare we say promising, aspects of this story is the role that investors have played in driving the creation of the Standard. Investor activism has emerged as a major force for social change in recent years. The role of investors in the GTR is part of that broader movement.

There are potentially 2 sets of motives now driving investor activism, the first is ethical or moral concerns, and the second is financial self-interest. Our aim here is to consider the role of these 2 sets of investor motives in driving the development of the Standard. As a preliminary matter, it will be useful to demonstrate these motivations in 2 contrasting cases, before we focus on the GTR. The first of these cases is investor activism in relation to climate change, where the motivation is a sophisticated form of financial self-interest. The second is the response of investors following Rio Tinto's destruction of Juukan Gorge rock shelters, a response that is driven primarily by ethical considerations.

Climate change

When climate change first emerged as an issue, it was generally assumed that its impact would be many generations into the future and not a matter of immediate concern to investors. It was an ethical issue about a burden that our current lifestyle was placing on anonymous generations to come. Mainstream fund managers therefore saw no need to respond. Concerned individuals tried to influence the investment policies of these fund managers, but with little success.

However, as time went on it became clear that the consequences of climate change were more immediate and would impact on our grandchildren or even our children. Finally, the consequences moved into the present. It is now clear that climate change has contributed to the extreme weather events we are currently experiencing, events that have massive financial consequences.

As climate change has unfolded, the public has become increasingly concerned and governments have enacted polices to reduce carbon-dioxide emissions, in particular, policies to curtail the use of fossil fuels and replace them with renewables. The result is that it has become increasingly risky, from a financial point of view, to invest in fossil fuel industries. Climate change has moved from being purely an ethical issue to a matter of financial self-interest for investors.[1]

There is now a likelihood that fossil fuel assets may end up "stranded", losing most if not all their value. The term "stranded asset" was introduced into the climate change debate by an Oxford University think tank, Carbon Tracker.[2] It has been seminal in concretising the financial risk of climate change in the mind of investors. As Carbon Tracker itself says, its research on stranded assets has resulted in "the embedding of climate change risk within conventional understanding of financial risk".[3]

Mainstream investor organisations are now very aware of this risk and are taking action. In Australia, several superannuation funds have committed to achieving net zero emission from their investment portfolios by 2050,[4] which brings them into alignment with the goals of the Paris 2015 agreement. In this respect, they are well ahead of the Australian Government which, at the time of writing, is only prepared to commit to reaching net zero during the second half of the century.

In January 2020, the CEO of BlackRock, the world's largest asset manager with nearly $7 trillion in investments, wrote to company CEOs in the following terms:

> "Climate change has become a defining factor in companies' long-term prospects... BlackRock [has] announced a number of initiatives to place sustainability at the center of our investment approach, including: making sustainability integral to portfolio construction and risk management; exiting investments that present a high sustainability-related risk, such as thermal coal producers; launching new investment products that screen fossil fuels".[5]

As these developments make clear, when it comes to climate change, many institutional investors are now committed to divestment from the most emissions-intensive industries for reasons of financial risk.

---

[1] Denis, A, Super funds are feeling the financial heat from climate change, *The Conversation*, 16 September 2020. theconversation.com/super-funds-are-feeling-the-financial-heat-from-climate-change-146191.

[2] Carbon Tracker, Stranded Assets, carbontracker.org/terms/stranded-assets/.

[3] carbontracker.org/about/.

[4] Denis, A, op cit.

[5] Fink, L, *A Fundamental Reshaping of Finance*, BlackRock CEO letter 2020. blackrock.com/corporate/investor-relations/larry-fink-ceo-letter.

They are also seeking to force change by using interventionist strategies that fall short of divestment. Climate Action 100+ represents a group of investors that collectively manage more than US$47 trillion in assets. In 2020, it wrote to 161 fossil fuel, mining, transport and other big-emitting companies requesting them to establish 30 climate measures and targets against which they will be assessed. This is part of a continuing campaign by climate-concerned shareholders to force business leaders to explain how their targets and strategies will help reach the goals of the 2015 Paris agreement.[6] This is a concerted effort by investors to influence the companies in which they invest.

These initiatives are having a profound effect on some fossil fuel companies. The petroleum company, BP, has committed to net zero carbon emissions by 2050. It will do this in part by cutting back substantially on its oil and gas production and increasing dramatically its investment in renewable energy. According to its CEO, he had 2 groups of people in mind when making this decision: employees and investors. Employees were concerned about the gap between their personal views about climate change and the company's purpose. As for the second group, "the sense that investors were really beginning to push, and question our purpose, started to weigh on the financial performance of our sector".[7] Other oil and gas companies are responding similarly.

In summary, the reaction of mainstream investor groups to climate change has been largely one of financial self-interest. It was only when climate change came to be seen as a financial risk that they began to take action.

Rio Tinto's destruction of aboriginal rock shelters

Consider now a contrasting case – investor reaction to Rio Tinto's destruction of the 46,000-year-old aboriginal heritage sites in the pursuit of profit, as described in Chapter 7. Rio Tinto's actions generated widespread community outrage, which led Rio Tinto to announce a so-called "independent" board-led review. The review was nothing of the sort; it was led by one of the non-executive directors of Rio Tinto. His report recommended that the "Rio trio", the company's CEO, the head of corporate relations and the head of Iron Ore in Australia, receives no bonus for the year. The company board agreed to this recommendation.

Rio Tinto's failure to conduct a truly independent review and the limited nature of the penalties imposed did nothing to assuage public outrage, it stoked it. What is significant here is that this outrage was articulated by big investors. Take the case of a peak industry body, the Australian Council of Superannuation Investors (ACSI) whose motto is to "research, engage, influence". Collectively, its members own, on average, 11% of each of the top 200 companies on the Australian Stock Exchange. Rio Tinto is one of the largest of those companies. The ACSI therefore speaks with the authority of an owner. It made the following public statement:[8]

> "The Australian Council of Superannuation Investors (ACSI) has noted the release by Rio Tinto of the board review into the destruction of culturally significant sites in the Juukan Gorge.

[6] Morton, A, Investors that manage US$47tn demand world's biggest polluters back plan for net-zero emissions, *The Guardian*, 14 September 2020. theguardian.com/environment/2020/sep/14/investors-worth-us47tn-demand-worlds-biggest-polluters-back-plan-for-net-zero-emissions.
[7] Walt, V, Is oil giant BP finally ready to 'think outside the barrel'?, *FORTUNE*, 10 August 2020. fortune.com/longform/bp-oil-gas-clean-energy-ceo-bernard-looney-petroleum-profits-stock/.
[8] Media release, 24 August 2020, acsi.org.au/media-releases/acsi-statement-on-rio-tinto-board-review-of-destruction-of-46000-year-old-caves-in-the-juukan-gorge/.

'The report from the Rio Tinto board review does not deliver any meaningful accountability for the destruction of some of the most significant cultural sites in Australia.' Said ACSI CEO Louise Davidson.

'The company should explain why greater accountability was not applied in light of this disaster.'

'Remuneration appears to be the only sanction applied to executives. This raises the question – does the company feel that £4 million is the right price for the destruction of cultural heritage?'

'An independent and transparent review would have given investors greater confidence that accountability applied was appropriate and proportionate.'"

This statement is a call for "greater accountability", which in this context means the sacking of the Rio trio. Several superannuation funds also made individual public statements deriding Rio Tinto's weak response.[9]

This was also a period of direct lobbying. ACSI and many other investors met with Rio Tinto executives to demand greater accountability.[10]

Rio Tinto's board was itself divided. At least 2 of its members believed that much stronger action was warranted.[11]

Ultimately, investor pressure proved decisive. The board reversed its earlier decision and forced the resignation of the trio of senior executives.

Following this decision, ACSI made another public statement:[12]

"ACSI CEO Louise Davidson said: 'Despite a drawn out process, we feel the Board has listened to investors and other stakeholders and taken appropriate steps to ensure executive accountability for the systemic failures that led to the disaster at Juukan Gorge.'

...

'Investors will continue to engage with Rio Tinto to understand how the company will manage this transition period. We will also be looking closely at the separation arrangements, with the expectation that any exit won't provide a windfall for executives on their departure.' She said".

Here, then, is a dramatic example of investor activism. In this case, the investor reaction went beyond protecting the financial interests of beneficiaries.[13] Rio Tinto's share price trended steadily upwards in the months following the destruction of the

---

[9] Verrender, I, Consequences for Rio Tinto over Juukan Gorge catastrophe are the new norm, *ABC News* 14 September 2020. abc.net.au/news/2020-09-14/superannuation-forcing-change-rio-tinto-juukan-gorge/12659824.

[10] ibid.

[11] Brummer, A, Rift between chairman Simon Thompson and 2 of Rio Tinto's most powerful independent directors presages a bumpy ride ahead. *Daily Mail* 18 September 2020. msn.com/en-gb/money/other/alex-brummer-rift-between-chairman-simon-thompson-and-two-of-rio-tintos-most-powerful-independent-directors-presages-a-bumpy-ride-ahead/ar-BB18INUN.

[12] ACSI, ACSI welcomes Rio Tinto changes, Media releases, 11 September 2020, acsi.org.au/media-releases/acsi-welcomes-rio-tinto-changes/.

[13] We make this statement notwithstanding the ASCI claim that "ESG (Environment Social and Governance) risks and opportunities have a material impact on investment outcomes", and that its members therefore have a fiduciary duty to take them into account. acsi.org.au/members/who-our-members-are/.

caves and investor funds were not at risk. Rio Tinto's behaviour was evidently an ethical question for investors. Their activism was driven by ethical concerns and not mere financial self-interest.

The global industry Standard

Consider now the involvement of investors in the development of a tailings management Standard. Recent tailings dam failures had killed hundreds of people and done immense environmental damage. Arguably, investors in mining companies have an ethical obligation to minimise the risk of such events. Tailings dam failures are also costly to investors, so institutional investors had a fiduciary (largely financial) duty to their beneficiaries to reduce the risk of failure.

This raises the following question. Were investor demands for a Standard primarily motivated by ethical concerns, or by financial self-interest, or were both important? The identity of the investor group in this case is a potential clue. As explained in Chapter 3, the Investor Mining and Tailings Safety Initiative was a subgroup of a larger group of companies that had signed up to the United Nations-sponsored "principles for responsible investment".[14] The first of these principles is this:

> "We will incorporate ESG (Environment, Social and Governance) issues into investment analysis and decision-making processes."

The other 5 principles are derivatives of this single principle and are redundant in the context of this chapter. Signatories publicly commit to adopt and implement these principles, "where consistent with our fiduciary responsibilities". The logic of this proviso is that where the principles of responsible investment conflict with the financial interests of fund beneficiaries, the principles will need to give way.

However, the leading funds in the investor tailings initiative, such as the Church of England Pensions Board, went further than this. Its policy is to invest in companies only if they comply with the board's ethical concerns. In the final analysis, it will divest from companies that fail this test,[15] even if they are providing a good return on investment. There is no doubt therefore that the investor group's demand for a Standard was at least in part motivated by ethical concerns.

Yet financial considerations were also at work. The *Financial Times* reports that shares in Vale dropped in value by 25% on the first day after the catastrophe.[16] They quickly recovered most of the lost value but have trended downwards ever since. Several institutional investors chose to divest from Vale after Brumadinho because they had "lost confidence" in the company or because they believed it had not implemented "sufficient measures" to prevent similar disasters. The language used was of "cutting exposure" to risk and the need to be "cautious" about investing in the mining sector, suggestive of a concern about financial as opposed to ethical risk. For these investors, the strategy was to divest.

---

[14] Principles for Responsible Investment (PRI), What are the Principles for Responsible Investment?, PRI. unpri.org/pri/what-are-the-principles-for-responsible-investment.

[15] The Church of England, Extractive Industries – The policy of the National Investing Bodies of the Church of England and the Ethical Investment Advisory Group's Advisory and Theological Papers, 2017. churchofengland.org/sites/default/files/2018-03/Extractive Industries Policy and Advice.pdf.

[16] Storbeck, O, Schipani, A, and Milne, R, Vale under pressure over safety as Union Investment sells stake, *Financial Times*, 8 April 2019. ft.com/content/308c0a20-579a-11e9-91f9-b6515a54c5b1.

If we refocus on the motivation of funds that pushed for the creation of the Standard, it is reasonable to conclude that they were driven by both ethical considerations and a desire to reduce the financial risk to which they were exposed.[17] These 2 motives together generate a credible threat of divestment if mining companies fail to meet investor expectations.

In summary, investor activism in relation to tailings dam failure is an example of a much broader phenomenon. This broader investor activism involves multiple motivations and multiple strategies, all of which are at work in the tailings case. When investors act collectively in this way, they can be a powerful force for social change, particularly in matters where governments cannot or will not lead the way.

The influence of the mining industry

While investors drove the decision to develop the Standard, it was the mining industry that largely controlled the process thereafter. There were at least 3 factors that, in combination, made industry the most influential of the 3 co-conveners during the development of the Standard:

■   knowledge asymmetry among the co-conveners

■   the industry capacity to mobilise

■   a willingness to bend or ignore the process established for the GTR.

Knowledge asymmetry among the co-conveners

Neither the PRI nor the United Nations Environment Program (UNEP) had a clear idea of what they wanted the Standard to contain. The mining industry, on the other hand, had a very clear idea of the kinds of requirements they would be prepared to sign up to and an equally clear idea of what they wanted excluded from the Standard. Moreover, industry had a detailed understanding of how tailings dams were constructed, while the other 2 groups did not. This meant that industry could simply argue that certain proposals were unrealistic and would make mining prohibitively expensive. Since all parties understood the importance of mining in the global economy and were committed to creating a Standard that would be implemented, this was a trump card that industry played from time to time very effectively. This very one-sided access to relevant knowledge placed industry in a powerful position. Investor groups and UNEP might have been able to exercise greater influence if they had been advised by geotechnical engineers and other tailings specialists with deep industry experience. But they did not draw on such advice, except in the final stage of the process, when UNEP's negotiating team included some technical advisors. This meant that throughout most of the process, the chief negotiators for UNEP and the PRI were unable to comment on much of the detail. They were therefore unable to act as advocates for various requirements that the expert panel proposed but to which industry objected.

---

17   Barrie, S, Baker, E, Howchin, J, and Matthews, A, Investor Mining and Tailings Safety Initiative, *GTR Compendium*, Chapter XVI. globaltailingsreview.org/wp-content/uploads/2020/09/Ch-XXVI-Investor-Mining-and-Tailings-Safety-Initiative.pdf.

Industry capacity to mobilise

The second reason the ICMM was such a powerful player was that it mobilised its resources, and that of its members, far more effectively than the other 2 co-conveners. The ICMM's senior executive officers were on the job from the very outset of the process almost continuously; they would have had very little time for anything else for many months. Furthermore, many of the company CEOs who sat on the ICMM council were actively involved in reviewing and amending the drafts produced by the expert panel, and later, involved in the ultimate negotiations with the investor and UNEP representatives. Finally, the CEOs had numerous technical advisors who combed through the various drafts and made numerous requests for changes. In short, the mining industry mobilised to protect its interests in a way that neither of the other 2 co-conveners did.

The failure to follow the agreed process.

A third reason the industry was able to exert so much influence is that it did not abide by the agreed process. The company CEOs on the Council never accepted the idea that the 3 co-conveners were equal. They behaved as if their interests were paramount and they expected the expert panel to do the same. They also failed to respect the independence of the chair and the panel, the most outstanding example of which was their insistence on modifying the draft Standard before it went out for public consultation. In contrast, the other 2 co-conveners stood back at this stage, and at several others, in order not to prejudice the independence of the process. In so doing, they made it possible for the ICMM to exert unopposed pressure on the panel.

These 3 factors go a long way towards explaining the disproportionate influence the ICMM had on the construction and content of the Standard.

The question of implementation

The final round in the contest between industry and the other 2 co-conveners concerns the question of how the Standard is to be implemented. At the time of writing, this contest is in its early stages and it remains to be seen how matters evolve. The balance of power may shift again at this stage. Despite a stated intent by the ICMM and its members to be more open and collaborative, we envisage that the establishment of the independent entity will be hotly contested. The industry will prefer to retain control of the Standard and will seek to slow down or stymie the establishment of the independent entity – knowing that without industry support, the entity is unlikely to be successful.

Failure to learn

One of the recurrent features of major accidents in hazardous industries is that the companies concerned have failed to identify and implement the lessons of previous disasters. So striking is this phenomenon that one of us (Hopkins) has written a book entitled *Failure to Learn*.[18] The relevant lessons are largely to do with how organisations operate.

---

[18] Hopkins, A, *Failure to Learn: The BP Texas City Refinery Disaster*, CCH Sydney, 2008.

This is true in relation to tailings dam disasters as well. Consider the Mount Polley tailings dam failure in the Canadian province of British Columbia in 2014. Apart from a company-commissioned report that was restricted to technical considerations, there was also a comprehensive report written by the inspectorate.[19]

The inspectorate's report identified a series of "root causes", all of which were organisational in nature. These included:

- production priorities prevailing over other considerations
- logistics limitations
- demand for increased tailings dam capacity
- no long-run planning
- no qualified person in charge of the facility
- no site integration
- insufficient management oversight
- a lack of any mechanism by which employees could escalate concerns.[20]

Of these, the report found that the most fundamental was the tendency for production to override all other considerations.

The expert panel managed to include requirements in the Standard that dealt with some of these issues. However, the ICMM repeatedly resisted requirements that were designed to deal with the most fundamental cause – the priority of production over all other considerations. Evidently, industry was unable or unwilling to learn the most fundamental lesson of the Mount Polley disaster.

The situation was similar with respect to the Brumadinho disaster. A preliminary report commissioned by the company was restricted to technical issues. A second and more comprehensive report (see Chapter 2) identified a series of organisational issues that contributed to the incident, among them:

- a failure to respond to warnings
- the co-option of supposedly independent auditors
- the lack of an independent risk function that bypasses business units, reports directly to the CEO and can act as an independent line of defence against failure
- the failure of senior executives to inform themselves effectively about how risk was being managed
- a bonus system that distracted attention from tailings facility safety.

This report was published on 20 February 2020, in English, in plenty of time to be absorbed by ICMM members before their final negotiations with the other

---

[19] British Columbia Chief Inspector of Mines, *Mount Polley Mine Tailings Storage Facility Breach, August 2014 – Investigation Report of the Chief Inspector of Mines*, Ministry of Mines and Energy, 30 November 2015. gov.bc.ca/assets/gov/farming-natural-resources-and-industry/mineral-exploration-mining/documents/directives-alerts-incidents/chief-inspector-s-report-page/m-200_mount_polley_2015-11-30_ci_investigation_report.pdf.

[20] op cit, pp 130, 137, 138, 141.

2 co-conveners. But the industry failed to modify its negotiating position to incorporate the lessons of Brumadinho into the final version of the Standard.

Various of the draft requirements that the ICMM had resisted or rejected were designed to deal with precisely the issues raised in these 2 reports. Depressingly, the industry showed no awareness of these connections. This is a classic example of the organisational failure to learn.

Multi-stakeholder initiatives

At the outset of the GTR, we did not envisage writing an insider account. Processes of industry reform are inevitably imperfect, requiring negotiation and compromise. The GTR was no different. However, on reflection, we felt compelled to document some of the internal dynamics as we saw them. While the industry can learn from past mistakes on tailings management, we can all learn how multi-stakeholder processes function in practice. This is important for ensuring that power disparities do not undermine either the process or the outcome. It is also important for ensuring that the voices of people who have suffered the most are not lost in the process. This book can therefore be seen as a contribution to the literature on multi-stakeholder initiatives to regulate corporate behaviour.[21]

Our original intent was to support a transparent multi-stakeholder process of industry reform. However, what we observed was an industry privately wielding its superior power to inhibit the reform process, while publicly representing the GTR as a collaboration of equals. It seemed to us that at too many points in the process, the mining industry was more intent on defending and controlling the outcome than on listening and learning. The public narrative of the process glosses over these political aspects. This was to some extent necessary at the outset in order to encourage the uptake of the new Standard. However, we also see benefit in offering an alternative narrative now that the uptake and implementation process is underway.

Multi-stakeholder initiatives are intended to build mutual understanding where there is a deficit of trust. The political analysis we have offered indicates that trust-building is an immensely difficult project and can be easily undermined, sometimes by the same parties that most want to earn it. The establishment of an independent entity to oversee the new Standard will be vital to the completion of this project and the ongoing process of industry reform.

---

[21] MSI Integrity and the Duke Human Rights Center at the Kenan Institute for Ethics, *The New Regulators? Assessing the Landscape of Multi-Stakeholder Initiatives*, June 2017. msi-integrity.org/dev/wp-content/uploads/2017/05/The-New-Regulators-MSI-Database-Report.pdf.

Postscript

On 18 December 2020, an announcement was made about the creation of an independent entity to oversee the Global Tailings Standard.[1] Our book was already in production at this time, hence this postscript.

The announcement was made by the United Nations Environment Programme (UNEP) and the 2 investment funds that led the Principles for Responsible Investment (PRI) during the Global Tailings Review — the Church of England Pensions Board and the Council on Ethics of the Swedish National Pension Funds.

UNEP and the PRI confirmed that they intended to establish an independent institute, a "home" for the Standard. The institute would enable the Standard to evolve over time and ensure its implementation "as intended" (although there was no indication that the entity would provide certification). The most tangible commitment in the announcement was that UNEP would recruit a consultant for 12 months to lead the process.

We are encouraged that an independent entity is to be formed and in fact we lend our support to this idea in the book. We are nonetheless discouraged by the conspicuous absence of the International Council for Mining and Metals (ICMM), or any of its member companies, in this important next step. While the development of the Standard had been a tripartite endeavour, it seems the institute will be bipartite only.

Whether the ICMM's absence is a rejection of the very idea of an independent entity, or an opportunity for UNEP and the PRI to safeguard the Standard from industry influence, remains to be seen. The real test, however, is what happens on the ground, in places where the industry extracts minerals and stores its waste. On this issue, actions must speak louder than words.

Matters will of course continue to develop in the coming months and years. We hope that, in the process, the numerous issues and concerns that we outline in this book will be taken into account.

---

[1] unep.org/news-and-stories/press-release/partnership-support-global-tailings-standard.

Appendix 1
The foundation document

Independent review of global best practices to inform an international standard on mine tailings storage facilities

A. Context and importance of independence

Context for the review

ICMM, PRI and UNEP share a commitment to the adoption of global best practices on tailings storage facilities. ICMM has committed to developing an international standard for tailings storage facilities for its member companies. The standard will be informed by and developed through an independent review of current global best practices in the mining industry, and beyond, and adherence to the standard will become part of the membership requirements of ICMM. The review will be co-convened by ICMM, PRI and UNEP. While the standard would become an ICMM company member commitment, the co-convening partners will encourage others to join in advocating for it to be adopted more broadly.

Ensuring process independence and integrity

How do we engage external parties in a manner that underscores the independence and integrity of the review process, and supports the delivery of a pragmatic, progressive, workable outcome that members will be willing to implement?

Working assumptions:

1. ICMM members are committed to a step change in performance (design, operation and closure) to restore the confidence of key stakeholders, including investors and host communities.
2. To be a credible process it needs to be multi stakeholder. A wholly industry-owned process will not be regarded as credible and will therefore serve no purpose.
3. Governance of the process is key to ensure independence as ICMM will have to fund the review, and its members will be involved in providing input,
4. The appointment of a Chair that is regarded as objective and impartial to oversee the work of an expert panel is a critical success factor.
5. The co-convenors are committed to engaging representatives from civil society, communities, industry, investors, and multilateral organisations, as well as engineers and subject matter experts, to determine the detailed scope of the review. Instilling confidence in stakeholders by considering their views is a critical success factor.
6. Providing a timely solution that member companies can move to implement is very important, so the stakeholder engagement parameters will benefit from risk prioritisation and a specified list of achievable outcomes.
7. The co-convenors are equally invested in achieving a workable outcome, to avoid inhibiting uptake and implementation by ICMM members or others within the industry.

B. Considerations for good governance of the review

1. ***Oversight by a limited number of co-convening parties with an equal say:*** ICMM will co-convene the review with two independent institutional partners: the Principles for Responsible Investment (PRI) and UN Environment Programme (UNEP). Key decisions relating to the overall process will need to be by mutual agreement between the three co-convenors. For example, all parties would need to be supportive of the choice for an independent Chair for the expert panel.

2. ***Autonomy of the Chair to effectively lead the review:*** The Chair will work with the co-convenors to appoint the expert panel and determine how the review will be conducted, based on a scope of work to be agreed with the co-convenors.

3. ***Active engagement of a diverse set of stakeholders:*** The co-convenors will agree on how to actively engage a diverse set of stakeholders (for example in an advisory capacity), but within defined Terms of Reference to be agreed by the co-convenors at a very early stage. The input of stakeholders will be advisory – in the first instance, to the co-convenors in determining the scope of the review, and subsequently to the Chair and expert panel in the conduct of the review.

4. ***Technical input from tailings experts in mining companies:*** The Chair and expert panel will also have access to technical expertise on tailings from across ICMM members. This group could be used as a resource to either solicit information on current management and governance practices, or as a sounding board for initial ideas that the expert panel may wish to test. Their involvement would be demand-driven rather than supply-driven.

C. Summary of proposed governance structure and key roles for each entity

1. Co-convenors.

Representatives: ICMM, PRI and UNEP

Roles:
- Define the governance of the review, including agreement on:
    1. Terms of reference for Chair
    2. Terms of reference for Advisory Group
    3. Schedule
- Select chair
- Select the expert panel
- Monitor progress
- Review and comment on the international standard to be developed, to ensure it is fit for purpose
- Review and comment on the draft report and recommendations

Likely time commitment: 2 x 1-day physical meetings, interviews of candidates for chair if needed, plus some time to review and comment on TOR and reports (10 - 15 days in total).

2. Chair

Senior, respected person who will be seen as independent. S/he will likely be a former employee of multilateral organisation, a former government minister, or some other person with demonstrated experience of chairing diverse groups to develop policy or standards, ideally complemented with senior (board level) experience in the private sector.

Roles (within agreed terms of reference per above):
- Select experts in accordance with qualification criteria
- Engage with Advisory Group to obtain their input prior to commencing work
- Determine review scope and work programme with experts
- Oversee report compilation
- Consult with Advisory Group on report and recommendations
- Run public online consultations and/or regional consultations as appropriate
- Consult with Co-Convenors on report and recommendations
- Finalise and present report

Likely time commitment: 90 – 140 days, spread over about 8 months.

Administrative and logistical support will be provided to the Chair.

3. Advisory Group

Representatives of important stakeholder groups tasked with providing advice to the Chair and expert panel comprising no more than 15 people representing the following categories:
- Human rights
- Community NGO
- Indigenous Peoples
- Labour
- Environmental NGOs
- Investors
- Insurers
- Multilateral Development Banks
- Tailings experts
- Mining associations
- Oversight institutions for global codes or standards

Roles:
Provide consultative input to the Chair and expert panel in an advisory capacity at key points in the process.

Likely time commitment: 10 days including feedback etc and including 2 meetings (possibly 3 if iteration needed)

4. Expert Panel

Representatives: no more than 7 technical experts with diverse range of disciplines (such as safety/risk analysis, tailings, organisational behaviour, (ex) regulator, community/social expert), selected in accordance with a pre-determined minimum list of qualifications.

Roles:
Execute agreed work programme and support chair in report compilation and responding to consultations

Likely time commitment: 45 to 60 days per expert over 6 to 8 months. A legal expert will either be on the panel or will provide advice to the panel.

5. Technical experts on tailings within ICMM members

Technical experts on tailings within ICMM member companies.

Roles:
This group could be used as a resource for the chair and panel of experts to either solicit information on current management and governance practices, or as a sounding board for initial ideas that the expert panel may wish to test.

Likely time commitment: As needs basis

D. Objective and scope of the review

Objective

To review current global best practices in the mining industry, and beyond, and based on this information develop an international standard that creates a step change for the industry in the safety and security of tailings storage facilities (TSFs).

Scope

Building on existing global best practices, the overall scope of the review will be determined by the need to inform the development of a standard that addresses, but is not limited to, the following:

- A global and transparent consequence-based TSF classification system with appropriate requirements for each level of classification.
- A system for credible, independent reviews of tailings storage facilities.
- Requirements for emergency planning and preparedness.

The first output of the review is an international standard that can practically be implemented to achieve the objective of the review. The review will also consider governance options to ensure uptake of and compliance with the standard. This output must enjoy the support of the three co-convenors.

The second output of the review is a report that outlines broader recommendations for the industry. The analysis of the behavioural, cultural, and structural factors listed below, which may not lead to specific provisions in the international standard, will inform these broader recommendations. The Chair is empowered to independently propose recommendations, and the parties subject to the recommendations will respond to them as appropriate

The detailed scope of the review will be refined through a process of engagement with representatives from communities, civil society, industry, investors, and multilateral organisations. However, it could focus on the following aspects:

Classification of TSFs:

- What classification systems already exist for TSFs and what are the perceived strengths and weaknesses of each?

- What relative weights is afforded to the consequences of failure in each of these classification systems and how does that translate into requirements for emergency planning and preparedness

- What are the public reporting/disclosure requirements associated with each classification system, to regulators and other stakeholders (including local communities and investors)?

- Broadly speaking, how effective have these classification systems been in preventing the failure of TSFs or mitigating their effects?

- What would a consequence-based TSF classification system look like, that could be practically applied irrespective of geographic location or the existing requirements of classification systems, and would be resilient to climate change?

- What would the requirements for independent review (see below) or emergency planning and preparedness look like for each classification category?

Independent review of TSFs:

- What independent review processes already exist for TSFs (e.g. independent tailings review boards, independent geotechnical review boards, engineers of record) and under what circumstances are these applied?

- What testing, monitoring and inspection regimes apply to TSFs, how do these relate to the design of the TSF (e.g. upstream, downstream, centreline), and to the requirements for independent review?

- What are the perceived strengths and weaknesses of existing independent review processes and testing and inspection regimes?

- What would the requirements for independent review look like for each classification category (see above)?

Behavioural, cultural, and structural factors:

- What are the cultural, behavioural and incentive barriers within companies that block better management of TSFs?

- What structures and mechanisms for learning and accountability exist in our own industry (e.g. TSM) and other industries (oil and gas, nuclear) and what could we learn from them?

- What are the formal and continuing education requirements, as well as training, that are available for those who manage TSFs, both within companies and externally?

- What are the structural causes of and possible remedies for the shortage of experts (inadequate indemnification, consultant industry consolidation)?

- How could companies better engage with communities about the possible consequences of failure, to encourage better preparedness?

- Since the release of ICMM's position statement on tailings governance, what changes have been instituted relating to the governance of tailings storage facilities, and is change management being better managed?

- How can company tailings experts be more "empowered through internal governance structures, and should a more rigorous "competent persons" approach be considered, similar to ore reserves sign off?

- What changes should be considered to enable significant risks relating to tailings storage facilities to be elevated to senior management, e.g. Executive Committee level?

Beyond the scope of the present review:

- The review (and associated standard) will not cover detailed technical design criteria for tailings dams which are already covered by organisations such as the International Commission on Large Dams (ICOLD).

- The review will not look to exclude certain technologies such as upstream TSFs from future use. However, it will extend to the considerations that should determine the choice of such technologies or their suitability

- Riverine, deep sea and non-tailings related storage of materials will not be included in this review.
- Standards for rehabilitation of affected areas will not be part of the review or the standard to be developed.

E. Timeframe for the review

Once the Chair and expert members of the panel have been appointed, the expectation is that the main deliverable of the review will be completed within 6 months. However, there may be additional work as part of a second phase to support implementation

Annex 1: Role Specification for the Chair

The Chair should be a senior, respected person who will be seen as independent. S/he will likely be a former employee of multilateral organisation, a former government minister, or some other person with demonstrated experience of chairing diverse groups to develop policy or standards, ideally complemented with senior (board level) experience in the private sector.

Roles of the Chair (within agreed terms of reference per above):

- Select experts in accordance with qualification criteria
- Engage with Advisory Group to obtain their input prior to commencing work
- Determine review scope and work programme with experts
- Oversee report compilation
- Consult with the Advisory Group and others at key points in the process and on the draft report and recommendations
- Consult with Co-Convenors on report and recommendations
- Finalise and present report

The qualification criteria for the Chair are the following:

1. With some technical background in or demonstrated exposure to oil and gas, nuclear, hydropower, or other capital-intensive industries with significant safety issues to manage
2. Understanding of the concerns of, and credibility with, broad constituency (communities, indigenous peoples, etc)
3. Not currently or recently connected to mining, which would be seen as compromising independence; although prior mining sector experience would be helpful.
4. Understanding of, or ideally experience working with, business/investor community
5. Experience in forging policies across multiple disciplines (through, for example, multilateral or governmental processes)
6. Ideally, but not essentially, with prior experience running a similar high-level independent review process (e.g. Rana Plaza, Bangladesh)

The Chair will need to be available till the end of 2019. As mentioned in Section C 2 above, the likely time commitment is 90 days, spread over about 8 months.

Interested and qualified individuals should contact Aidan Davy, COO of ICMM, at aidan.davy@icmm.com, with a copy to John Howchin, Secretary General, The Council on Ethics for Sweden's AP Funds, at john.howchin@councilonethics.org, and Elisa Tonda, Head, Consumption and Production Unit, Economy Division, at elisa.tonda@un.org.

Source: https://globaltailingsreview.org/wp-content/uploads/2019/06/190604_GTR_governance-and-scope.pdf

Appendix 2
Key dates

4 August 2014	Mt Polley disaster
5 November 2015	Samarco disaster
25 January 2019	Brumadinho disaster
31 January 2019	PRI calls for standard
26 February 2019	ICMM announces commitment to Standard
21-22 June 2019	First expert panel meeting
14 November 2019	Red-lining by CEOs
15 November 2019	Launch of public consultation draft of Standard
20 February 2020	Publication of the Northfleet report on the Brumadinho failure
10 March 2020	Expert panel submits its final draft to co-conveners for consideration
18 May 2020	First meeting of 3 co-conveners
24 May 2020	Destruction of Juukan Gorge rock shelters
27 May 2020	Second meeting of 3 co-conveners
5 August 2020	Launch of Standard

Appendix 3

The Global Industry Standard on Tailings Management

Source: https://globaltailingsreview.org/wp-content/uploads/2020/08/global-industry-standard_EN.pdf.

GLOBAL INDUSTRY STANDARD ON TAILINGS MANAGEMENT

AUGUST 2020

CONTENT

PREAMBLE

The Global Industry Standard on Tailings Management (herein 'the Standard') strives to achieve the ultimate goal of zero harm to people and the environment with zero tolerance for human fatality. It requires *Operators* to take responsibility and prioritise the safety of *tailings facilities*, through all phases of a facility's *lifecycle*, including closure and post-closure. It also requires the disclosure of relevant information to support public accountability.

Issues have arisen in the development of the Standard that are difficult to translate into an auditable industry Standard for *Operators*. These issues are more appropriately addressed through national and/or state level regulatory authorities, or through multilateral agencies working with the industry. For example, it is recognised that more work needs to be done by national and/or state level regulators to develop mechanisms that enable the identification, maintenance and/or *restoration* of abandoned or 'orphaned' *facilities*.

The Standard provides a framework for safe *tailings facility* management while affording *Operators* flexibility as to how best to achieve this goal. For auditing and certification purposes, the Standard includes the Preamble, the Requirements, the Glossary and Annexes. Unless otherwise specified, the Requirements of the Standard are directed to the *Operator*. The Requirements apply to individual facilities as defined in the Glossary, and are all intended to apply and be auditable.

Conformance with the Standard does not displace the requirements of any specific national, state or local governmental statutes, laws, regulations, ordinances, or other government directives. *Operators* are expected to conform with the Requirements of the Standard not in conflict with other provisions of law.

The Standard will be supported by implementation protocols which will provide detailed guidance for certification, or assurance as applicable, and for equivalence with other standards. Many activities referenced in this Standard may be found as part of a comprehensive mine-wide *environmental and social management system*. Where credible systems for assuring these requirements are already in place (such as third party audit or verification processes), these should be recognised as equivalent to avoid duplication, to the extent reasonably practicable.

Although the Standard follows a logical sequence arranged around broad topic areas, the Requirements are not presented chronologically. The Principles are intended to summarise the Requirements that follow and are not in themselves auditable. To reduce repetition, the disclosure requirements are grouped under Principle 15. These Requirements support public accountability and protect *Operators* from the need to disclose confidential commercial or financial information.

All terms that appear in *italics* are defined in the Glossary, Annex 1.

GLOBAL INDUSTRY STANDARD ON TAILINGS MANAGEMENT

ACRONYMS

CDIV	Construction versus Design Intent Verification
DBR	Design Basis Report
DSR	Dam Safety Review
EOR	Engineer of Record
EPRP	Emergency Preparedness and Response Plan
ESMS	Environmental and Social Management System
FPIC	Free Prior and Informed Consent
GTR	Global Tailings Review
ICMM	International Council on Mining and Metals
ICOLD	International Commission on Large Dams
IFC	International Finance Corporation
ITRB	Independent Tailings Review Board
OMS	Operations, Maintenance and Surveillance
PRI	Principles for Responsible Investment
RTFE	Responsible Tailings Facility Engineer
TARP	Triggered Action Response Plan
TMS	Tailings Management System
UNEP	United Nations Environment Programme
UNGP	United Nations Guiding Principles on Business and Human Rights

AFFECTED COMMUNITIES
TOPIC I

PRINCIPLE 1   RESPECT THE RIGHTS OF *PROJECT-AFFECTED PEOPLE* AND *MEANINGFULLY ENGAGE* THEM AT ALL PHASES OF THE *TAILINGS FACILITY LIFECYCLE*, INCLUDING CLOSURE.

Requirement 1.1   Demonstrate respect for human rights in accordance with the United Nations Guiding Principles on Business and Human Rights (UNGP), conduct human rights due diligence to inform management decisions throughout the *tailings facility lifecycle* and address the human rights risks of *tailings facility credible failure scenarios*.

For existing facilities, the *Operator* can initially opt to prioritise salient human rights issues in accordance with the UNGP.

Requirement 1.2   Where a new *tailings facility* may impact the rights of indigenous or tribal peoples, including their land and resource rights and their right to self-determination, work to obtain and maintain *Free Prior and Informed Consent (FPIC)* by demonstrating conformance to international guidance and recognised *best practice* frameworks.

Requirement 1.3   Demonstrate that *project-affected people* are *meaningfully engaged* throughout the *tailings facility lifecycle* in building the *knowledge base* and in decisions that may have a bearing on public safety and the integrity of the *tailings facility*. The *Operator* shall share information to support this process.

Requirement 1.4   Establish an effective operational-level, non-judicial *grievance* mechanism that addresses complaints and *grievances* of *project-affected people* relating to the *tailings facility*, and provide remedy in accordance with the UNGP.

INTEGRATED KNOWLEDGE BASE
TOPIC II

PRINCIPLE 2	**DEVELOP AND MAINTAIN AN INTERDISCIPLINARY *KNOWLEDGE BASE* TO SUPPORT SAFE *TAILINGS* MANAGEMENT THROUGHOUT THE *TAILINGS FACILITY LIFECYCLE*, INCLUDING CLOSURE.**

Requirement 2.1   Develop and document knowledge about the social, environmental and local economic context of the *tailings facility*, using approaches aligned with international *best practices*. Update this knowledge at least every five years, and whenever there is a *material* change either to the *tailings facility* or to the social, environmental and local economic context. This knowledge should capture uncertainties due to climate change.

Requirement 2.2   Prepare, document and update a detailed site characterisation of the *tailings facility* site(s) that includes data on climate, geomorphology, geology, geochemistry, hydrology and hydrogeology (surface and groundwater flow and quality), geotechnical, and seismicity. The physical and chemical properties of the *tailings* shall be characterised and updated regularly to account for variability in ore properties and processing.

Requirement 2.3   Develop and document a *breach analysis* for the *tailings facility* using a methodology that considers *credible failure modes*, site conditions, and the properties of the slurry. The results of the analysis shall estimate the physical area impacted by a potential failure. When flowable materials (water and liquefiable solids) are present at *tailings facilities* with Consequence Classification of 'High', 'Very High' or 'Extreme', the results should include estimates of the physical area impacted by a potential failure, flow arrival times, depth and velocities, and depth of material deposition. Update whenever there is a *material* change either to the *tailings facility* or the physical area impacted.

Requirement 2.4   In order to identify the groups most at risk, refer to the updated *tailings facility breach analysis* to assess and document potential human exposure and vulnerability to *tailings facility credible failure scenarios*. Update the assessment whenever there is a *material* change either to the *tailings facility* or to the *knowledge base*.

PRINCIPLE 3	USE ALL ELEMENTS OF THE *KNOWLEDGE BASE* - SOCIAL, ENVIRONMENTAL, LOCAL ECONOMIC AND TECHNICAL - TO INFORM DECISIONS THROUGHOUT THE *TAILINGS FACILITY LIFECYCLE*, INCLUDING CLOSURE.
Requirement 3.1	To enhance resilience to climate change, evaluate, regularly update and use climate change knowledge throughout the *tailings facility lifecycle* in accordance with the principles of *Adaptive Management*.
Requirement 3.2	For new *tailings facilities*, the *Operator* shall use the *knowledge base* and undertake a multi-criteria *alternatives analysis* of all feasible sites, technologies and strategies for *tailings* management. The goal of this analysis shall be to: (i) select an alternative that minimises risks to people and the environment throughout the *tailings facility lifecycle*; and (ii) minimise the volume of *tailings* and water placed in external *tailings facilities*. This analysis shall be reviewed by the *Independent Tailings Review Board (ITRB)* or a *senior independent technical reviewer*. For existing *tailings facilities*, the *Operator* shall periodically review and refine the *tailings* technologies and design, and management strategies to minimise risk and improve environmental outcomes. An exception applies to facilities that are demonstrated to be in a state of *safe closure*.
Requirement 3.3	For new *tailings* facilities, use the *knowledge base*, including uncertainties due to climate change, to assess the social, environmental and local economic impacts of the *tailings facility* and its potential failure throughout its *lifecycle*. Where *impact assessments* predict *material* acute or chronic impacts, the *Operator* shall develop, document and implement impact mitigation and management plans using the *mitigation hierarchy*.
Requirement 3.4	Update the assessment of the social, environmental and local economic impacts to reflect a *material* change either to the *tailings facility* or to the social, environmental and local economic context. If new data indicates that the impacts from the *tailings facility* have changed *materially*, including as a result of climate change knowledge or long-term impacts, the *Operator* shall update *tailings facility* management to reflect the new data using *Adaptive Management best practices*.

DESIGN, CONSTRUCTION, OPERATION AND MONITORING OF THE TAILINGS FACILITY

TOPIC III

PRINCIPLE 4   DEVELOP PLANS AND DESIGN CRITERIA FOR THE *TAILINGS FACILITY* TO MINIMISE RISK FOR ALL PHASES OF ITS *LIFECYCLE,* INCLUDING CLOSURE AND POST-CLOSURE.

Requirement 4.1   Determine the consequence of failure classification of the *tailings facility* by assessing the downstream conditions documented in the *knowledge base* and selecting the classification corresponding to the highest Consequence Classification for each category in Annex 2, Table 1. The assessment and selection of the classification shall be based on *credible failure modes*, and shall be defensible and documented.

Requirement 4.2   With the objective of maintaining flexibility in the development of a new *tailings facility* and optimising costs while prioritising safety throughout the *tailings facility lifecycle*:

A. Develop *preliminary designs* for the *tailings facility* with external loading design criteria consistent with both the consequence of failure classification selected based on current conditions and higher Consequence Classifications (including 'Extreme').

B. Informed by the range of requirements defined by the *preliminary designs*, either:

1. Implement the design for the 'Extreme' Consequence Classification external loading criteria; or
2. Implement the design for the current Consequence Classification criteria, or a higher one, and demonstrate that the feasibility, at a proof of concept level, to upgrade to the design for the 'Extreme' classification criteria is maintained throughout the *tailings facility lifecycle*.

C. If option B.2 is implemented, review the consequence of failure classification at the time of the *Dam Safety Review (DSR)* and at least every five years, or sooner if there is a *material* change in the social, environmental and local economic context, and complete the upgrade of the *tailings facility* to the new Consequence Classification as determined by the *DSR* within three years. This review shall proceed until the *tailings facility* has been *safely closed* according to this Standard.

D. The process described above shall be reviewed by the *Independent Tailings Review Board (ITRB)* or the *senior independent technical reviewer,* as appropriate for the *tailings facility* Consequence Classification.

Subject to Requirement 4.7, Requirements 4.2.C and 4.2.D shall also apply to existing *tailings facilities*.

Requirement 4.3   The *Accountable Executive* shall take the decision to adopt a design for the current Consequence Classification criteria and to maintain flexibility to upgrade the design for the highest classification criteria later in the *tailings facility lifecycle*. This decision shall be documented.

Requirement 4.4   Select, explicitly identify and document all design criteria that are appropriate to minimise risk for all *credible failure modes* for all phases of the *tailings facility lifecycle*.

Requirement 4.5   Apply design criteria, such as factors of safety for slope stability and seepage management, that consider estimated operational properties of materials and expected performance of design elements, and quality of the implementation of risk management systems. These issues should also be appropriately accounted for in designs based on deformation analyses.

Requirement 4.6   Identify and address brittle failure modes with conservative design criteria, independent of trigger mechanisms, to minimise their impact on the performance of the *tailings facility*.

Requirement 4.7   Existing *tailings facilities* shall conform with the Requirements under Principle 4, except for those aspects where the *Engineer of Record (EOR)*, with review by the *ITRB* or a *senior independent technical reviewer*, determines that the upgrade of an existing *tailings facility* is not viable or cannot be retroactively applied. In this case, the *Accountable Executive* shall approve and document the implementation of measures to reduce both the probability and the consequences of a *tailings facility* failure in order to reduce the risk to a level *as low as reasonably practicable (ALARP)*. The basis and timing for addressing the upgrade of existing *tailings facilities* shall be risk-informed and carried out as soon as reasonably practicable.

Requirement 4.8   The *EOR* shall prepare a *Design Basis Report (DBR)* that details the design assumptions and criteria, including operating constraints, and that provides the basis for the design of all phases of the *tailings facility lifecycle*. The *DBR* shall be reviewed by the *ITRB* or *senior independent technical reviewer*. The *EOR* shall update the *DBR* every time there is a *material* change in the design assumptions, design criteria, design or the *knowledge base* and confirm internal consistency among these elements.

PRINCIPLE 5   DEVELOP A *ROBUST DESIGN* THAT INTEGRATES THE *KNOWLEDGE BASE* AND MINIMISES THE RISK OF FAILURE TO PEOPLE AND THE ENVIRONMENT FOR ALL PHASES OF THE *TAILINGS FACILITY LIFECYCLE*, INCLUDING CLOSURE AND POST-CLOSURE.

Requirement 5.1   For new *tailings facilities*, incorporate the outcome of the multi-criteria *alternatives analysis* including the use of *tailings* technologies in the design of the *tailings facility*.

For expansions to existing *tailings facilities*, investigate the potential to refine the *tailings* technologies and design approaches with the goal of minimising risks to people and the environment throughout the *tailings facility lifecycle*.

Requirement 5.2   Develop a *robust design* that considers the technical, social, environmental and local economic context, the *tailings facility* Consequence Classification, site conditions, water management, mine plant operations, *tailings* operational and construction issues, and that demonstrates the feasibility of *safe closure* of the *tailings* facility. The design should be reviewed and updated as performance and site data become available and in response to *material* changes to the *tailings facility* or its performance.

Requirement 5.3   Develop, implement and maintain a water balance model and associated water management plans for the *tailings facility*, taking into account the *knowledge base* including climate change, upstream and downstream hydrological and hydrogeological basins, the mine site, mine planning and overall operations and the integrity of the *tailings facility* throughout its *lifecycle*. The water management programme must be designed to protect against unintentional releases.

Requirement 5.4   Address all potential failure modes of the structure, its foundation, abutments, reservoir (*tailings* deposit and pond), reservoir rim and appurtenant structures to minimise risk to *ALARP*. Risk assessments must be used to inform the design.

Requirement 5.5   Develop a design for each stage of construction of the *tailings facility*, including but not limited to start-up, partial raises and interim configurations, final raise, and all closure stages.

Requirement 5.6   Design the closure phase in a manner that meets all the Requirements of the Standard with sufficient detail to demonstrate the feasibility of the closure scenario and to allow implementation of elements of the design during construction and operation as appropriate. The design should include progressive closure and *reclamation* during operations.

Requirement 5.7   For a proposed new *tailings facility* classified as 'High', 'Very High' or 'Extreme', the *Accountable Executive* shall confirm that the design satisfies *ALARP* and shall approve additional *reasonable steps* that may be taken downstream, to further reduce potential consequences to people and the environment. The *Accountable Executive* shall explain and document the decisions with respect to *ALARP* and additional consequence reduction measures.

For an existing *tailings facility* classified as 'High', 'Very High' or 'Extreme', the *Accountable Executive*, at the time of every *DSR* or at least every five years, shall confirm that the design satisfies *ALARP* and shall seek to identify and implement additional *reasonable steps* that may be taken to further reduce potential consequences to people and the environment. The *Accountable Executive* shall explain and document the decisions with respect to *ALARP* and additional consequence reduction measures, in consultation with external parties as appropriate.

Requirement 5.8   Where other measures to reduce the consequences of a *tailings facility credible failure* mode as per the *breach analysis* have been exhausted, and pre-emptive resettlement cannot be avoided, the Operator shall demonstrate conformance with international standards for *involuntary resettlement*.

PRINCIPLE 6   PLAN, BUILD AND OPERATE THE *TAILINGS FACILITY* TO MANAGE RISK AT
                     ALL PHASES OF THE *TAILINGS FACILITY LIFECYCLE*, INCLUDING CLOSURE
                     AND POST-CLOSURE

Requirement 6.1   Build, operate, monitor and close the *tailings facility* according to the
                     design intent at all phases of the *tailings facility lifecycle*, using qualified
                     personnel and appropriate methodology, equipment and procedures, data
                     acquisition methods, the *Tailings Management System (TMS)* and the overall
                     Environmental and Social Management System (ESMS) for the mine and
                     associated infrastructure.

Requirement 6.2   Manage the quality and adequacy of the construction and operation process
                     by implementing Quality Control, Quality Assurance and *Construction
                     vs Design Intent Verification (CDIV)*. The *Operator* shall use the *CDIV* to
                     ensure that the design intent is implemented and is still being met if the site
                     conditions vary from the design assumptions.

Requirement 6.3   Prepare a detailed *Construction Records Report* ('as-built' report) whenever
                     there is a *material* change to the *tailings facility*, its infrastructure or its
                     monitoring system. The *EOR* and the *Responsible Tailings Facility Engineer
                     (RTFE)* shall sign this report.

Requirement 6.4   Develop, implement, review annually and update as required an *Operations,
                     Maintenance and Surveillance (OMS) Manual* that supports effective risk
                     management as part of the *TMS*. The *OMS Manual* should follow *best
                     practices*, clearly provide the context and *critical controls* for safe operations,
                     and be reviewed for effectiveness. The *RTFE* shall provide access to the *OMS
                     Manual* and training to all levels of personnel involved in the *TMS* with support
                     from the *EOR*.

Requirement 6.5   Implement a formal *change management system* that triggers the evaluation,
                     review, approval and documentation of changes to design, construction,
                     operation or monitoring during the *tailings facility lifecycle*. The *change
                     management system* shall also include the requirement for the *EOR* to
                     prepare a periodic *Deviance Accountability Report (DAR)*, that provides an
                     assessment of the cumulative impact of the changes on the risk level of the
                     as-constructed facility. The *DAR* shall provide recommendations for managing
                     risk, if necessary, and any resulting updates to the design, *DBR*, *OMS* and
                     the monitoring programme. The *DAR* shall be approved by the *Accountable
                     Executive*.

Requirement 6.6   Include new and emerging technologies and approaches and use the evolving
                     knowledge in the refinement of the design, construction and operation of the
                     tailings facility.

PRINCIPLE 7   **DESIGN, IMPLEMENT AND OPERATE MONITORING SYSTEMS TO MANAGE RISK AT ALL PHASES OF THE FACILITY LIFECYCLE, INCLUDING CLOSURE.**

Requirement 7.1   Design, implement and operate a comprehensive and integrated performance monitoring programme for the *tailings facility* and its appurtenant structures as part of the *TMS* and for those aspects of the *ESMS* related to the *tailings facility* in accordance with the principles of *Adaptive Management*.

Requirement 7.2   Design, implement and operate a comprehensive and integrated engineering monitoring system that is appropriate for verifying design assumptions and for monitoring potential failure modes. Full implementation of the *Observational Method* shall be adopted for non-brittle failure modes. Brittle failure modes are addressed by conservative design criteria.

Requirement 7.3   Establish specific and measurable performance objectives, indicators, criteria, and performance parameters and include them in the design of the monitoring programmes that measure performance throughout the *tailings facility lifecycle*. Record and evaluate the data at appropriate frequencies. Based on the data obtained, update the monitoring programmes throughout the *tailings facility lifecycle* to confirm that they remain effective to manage risk.

Requirement 7.4   Analyse technical monitoring data at the frequency recommended by the *EOR*, and assess the performance of the *tailings facility*, clearly identifying and presenting evidence on any deviations from the expected performance and any deterioration of the performance over time. Promptly submit evidence to the *EOR* for review and update the risk assessment and design, if required. Performance outside the expected ranges shall be addressed promptly through *Trigger Action Response Plans (TARPs)* or *critical controls*.

Requirement 7.5   Report the results of each of the monitoring programmes at the frequency required to meet company and regulatory requirements and, at a minimum, on an annual basis. The *RTFE* and the *EOR* shall review and approve the technical monitoring reports.

MANAGEMENT AND GOVERNANCE

TOPIC IV

PRINCIPLE 8	**ESTABLISH POLICIES, SYSTEMS AND ACCOUNTABILITIES TO SUPPORT THE SAFETY AND INTEGRITY OF THE *TAILINGS FACILITY*.**
Requirement 8.1	The *Board of Directors* shall adopt and publish a policy on or commitment to the safe management of *tailings facilities*, to emergency preparedness and response, and to recovery after failure.
Requirement 8.2	Establish a *tailings governance framework* and a performance based *TMS* and ensure that the *ESMS* and other critical systems encompass relevant aspects of the *tailings facility* management.
Requirement 8.3	For roles with responsibility for *tailings facilities*, develop mechanisms such that incentive payments or performance reviews are based, at least in part, on public safety and the integrity of the *tailings facility*. These incentive payments shall reflect the degree to which public safety and the integrity of the *tailings facility* are part of the role. Long-term incentives for relevant executive managers should take *tailings* management into account.
Requirement 8.4	Appoint one or more *Accountable Executives* who is/are directly answerable to the CEO on matters related to this Standard. The *Accountable Executive(s)* shall be accountable for the safety of *tailings facilities* and for avoiding or minimising the social and environmental consequences of a *tailings facility* failure. The *Accountable Executive(s)* shall also be accountable for a programme of *tailings* management training, and for emergency preparedness and response. The *Accountable Executive(s)* must have scheduled communication with the *EOR* and regular communication with the *Board of Directors*, which can be initiated either by the *Accountable Executive(s)*, or the Board. The *Board of Directors* shall document how it holds the *Accountable Executive(s)* accountable.
Requirement 8.5	Appoint a site-specific *Responsible Tailings Facility Engineer (RTFE)* who is accountable for the integrity of the *tailings facility*, who liaises with the *EOR* and internal teams such as operations, planning, regulatory affairs, social performance and environment, and who has regular two-way communication with the *Accountable Executive*. The *RTFE* must be familiar with the *DBR*, the design report and the construction and performance of the *tailings facility*.
Requirement 8.6	Identify appropriate qualifications and experience requirements for all personnel who play safety-critical roles in the operation of a *tailings facility*, including, but not limited to the *RTFE*, the *EOR* and the *Accountable Executive*. Ensure that incumbents of these roles have the identified qualifications and experience, and develop succession plans for these personnel.
Requirement 8.7	For *tailings facilities* with Consequence Classification of 'Very High' or 'Extreme', appoint an *Independent Tailings Review Board (ITRB)*. For all other facilities, the *Operator* may appoint a *senior independent technical reviewer*. The *ITRB* or the reviewer shall be appointed early in the project development process, report to the *Accountable Executive* and certify in writing that they follow *best practices* for engineers in avoiding conflicts of interest.

PRINCIPLE 9   APPOINT AND EMPOWER AN *ENGINEER OF RECORD*.

Requirement 9.1   Engage an engineering firm with expertise and experience in the design and construction of *tailings facilities* of comparable complexity to provide *EOR* services for operating the *tailings facility* and for closed facilities with 'High', 'Very High' and 'Extreme' Consequence Classification, that are in the active closure phase. Require that the firm nominate a senior engineer, approved by the *Operator*, to represent the firm as the *EOR*, and verify that the individual has the necessary experience, skills and time to fulfil this role. Alternatively, the *Operator* may appoint an in-house engineer with expertise and experience in comparable facilities as the *EOR*. In this instance, the *EOR* may delegate the design to a firm ('*Designer of Record*') but shall remain thoroughly familiar with the design in discharging their responsibilities as *EOR*. Whether the *EOR* or the *DOR* is in-house or external, they must be competent and have experience appropriate to the Consequence Classification and complexity of the *tailings facility*.

Requirement 9.2   Empower the *EOR* through a written agreement that clearly describes their authority, role and responsibilities throughout the *tailings facility lifecycle*, and during change of ownership of mining properties. The written agreement must clearly describe the obligations of the *Operator* to the *EOR*, to support the effective performance of the *EOR*.

Requirement 9.3   Establish and implement a programme to manage the quality of all engineering work, the interactions between the *EOR*, the *RTFE* and the *Accountable Executive*, and their involvement in the *tailings facility lifecycle* as necessary to confirm that both the implementation of the design and the design intent are met.

Requirement 9.4   Given its potential impact on the risks associated with a *tailings facility*, the selection of the *EOR* shall be decided by the *Accountable Executive* and informed, but not decided, by procurement personnel.

Requirement 9.5   Where it becomes necessary to change the *EOR* (whether a firm or an in-house employee), develop a detailed plan for the comprehensive transfer of data, information, knowledge and experience with the construction procedures and materials.

PRINCIPLE 10	**ESTABLISH AND IMPLEMENT LEVELS OF REVIEW AS PART OF A STRONG QUALITY AND RISK MANAGEMENT SYSTEM FOR ALL PHASES OF THE *TAILINGS FACILITY LIFECYCLE*, INCLUDING CLOSURE.**
Requirement 10.1	Conduct and update risk assessments with a qualified multi-disciplinary team using *best practice* methodologies at a minimum every three years and more frequently whenever there is a *material* change either to the *tailings facility* or to the social, environmental and local economic context. Transmit risk assessments to the *ITRB* or *senior independent technical reviewer* for review, and address with urgency all unacceptable *tailings facility* risks.
Requirement 10.2	Conduct regular reviews of the *TMS* and of the components of the *ESMS* that refer to the *tailings facility* to assure the effectiveness of the management systems. Document and report the outcomes to the *Accountable Executive*, *Board of Directors* and *project-affected people*. The review shall be undertaken by *senior technical reviewers* with the appropriate qualifications, expertise and resources. For *tailings facilities* with 'High', 'Very High' or 'Extreme' Consequence Classification, conduct the review at least every three years.
Requirement 10.3	Conduct internal audits to verify consistent implementation of company procedures, guidelines and *corporate governance* requirements consistent with the *TMS* and aspects of the *ESMS* developed to manage *tailings facility risks*.
Requirement 10.4	The *EOR* or *senior independent technical reviewer* shall conduct *tailings facility* construction and performance reviews annually or more frequently, if required.
Requirement 10.5	Conduct an independent *DSR* at least every five years for *tailings facilities* with 'Very High' or 'Extreme' Consequence Classifications and at least every 10 years for all other *facilities*. For *tailings facilities* with complex conditions or performance, the *ITRB* may recommend more frequent *DSRs*. The *DSR* shall include technical, operational and *governance* aspects of the *tailings facility* and shall be completed according to *best practices*. The *DSR* contractor cannot conduct consecutive *DSRs* on the same *tailings facility* and shall certify in writing that they follow *best practices* for engineers in avoiding conflicts of interest.

Requirement 10.6   For *tailings facilities* with 'Very High' or 'Extreme' Consequence Classifications, the *ITRB*, reporting to the *Accountable Executive* shall provide ongoing senior independent review of the planning, siting, design, construction, operation, water and mass balance, maintenance, monitoring, performance and risk management at appropriate intervals across all phases of the *tailings facility lifecycle*. For *tailings facilities* with other Consequence Classifications, this review can be done by a *senior independent technical reviewer*.

Requirement 10.7   The amount of estimated costs for planned closure, early closure, *reclamation*, and post-closure of the *tailings facility* and its appurtenant structures shall be reviewed periodically to confirm that adequate financial capacity (including insurance, to the extent commercially reasonable) is available for such purposes throughout the *tailings facility lifecycle*, and the conclusions of the review shall be publicly disclosed annually. Disclosure may be made in audited financial statements or in public regulatory filings.

Subject to the provisions of local or national regulations on this matter, *Operators* shall use best efforts to assess and take into account the capability of an acquirer of any of its assets involving a *tailings facility* (through merger, acquisition, or other change in ownership) to maintain this Standard for the *tailings facility lifecycle*.

PRINCIPLE 11	DEVELOP AN ORGANISATIONAL CULTURE THAT PROMOTES LEARNING, COMMUNICATION AND EARLY PROBLEM RECOGNITION.
Requirement 11.1	Educate personnel who have a role in any phase of the *tailings facility lifecycle* about how their job procedures and responsibilities relate to the prevention of a failure.
Requirement 11.2	Establish mechanisms that incorporate workers' experience-based knowledge into planning, design and operations for all phases of the *tailings facility lifecycle*.
Requirement 11.3	Establish mechanisms that promote *cross-functional* collaboration to ensure effective data and knowledge sharing, communication and implementation of management measures to support public safety and the integrity of the *tailings facility*.
Requirement 11.4	Identify and implement lessons from internal incident investigations and relevant external incident reports, paying particular attention to human and organisational factors.
Requirement 11.5	Establish mechanisms that recognise, reward and protect from retaliation, employees and contractors who report problems or identify opportunities for improving *tailings facility* management. Respond in a timely manner and communicate actions taken and their outcomes.

PRINCIPLE 12	ESTABLISH A PROCESS FOR REPORTING AND ADDRESSING CONCERNS AND IMPLEMENT WHISTLEBLOWER PROTECTIONS.
Requirement 12.1	The *Accountable Executive* shall establish a formal, confidential and written process to receive, investigate and promptly address concerns from employees and contractors about possible permit violations or other matters relating to regulatory compliance, public safety, *tailings facility* integrity or the environment.
Requirement 12.2	In accordance with international *best practices* for whistleblower protection, the *Operator* shall not discharge, discriminate against, or otherwise retaliate in any way against a whistleblower who, in good faith, has reported possible permit violations or other matters relating to regulatory compliance, public safety, *tailings facility* integrity or the environment.

EMERGENCY RESPONSE AND LONG-TERM RECOVERY

TOPIC V

PRINCIPLE 13   PREPARE FOR EMERGENCY RESPONSE TO *TAILINGS FACILITY* FAILURES.

Requirement 13.1   As part of the *TMS*, use *best practices* and emergency response expertise to prepare and implement a site-specific tailings facility *Emergency Preparedness and Response Plan (EPRP)* based on *credible flow failure scenarios* and the assessment of potential consequences. Test and update the *EPRP* at all phases of the *tailings facility lifecycle* at a frequency established in the plan, or more frequently if triggered by a *material* change either to the *tailings facility* or to the social, environmental and local economic context. *Meaningfully engage* with employees and contractors to inform the *EPRP*, and co-develop community-focused emergency preparedness measures with *project-affected people.*

Requirement 13.2   Engage with *public sector agencies,* first responders, local authorities and institutions and take *reasonable* steps to assess the capability of emergency response services to address the *hazards* identified in the *tailings facility EPRP*, identify gaps in capability and use this information to support the development of a collaborative plan to improve preparedness.

Requirement 13.3   Considering community-focused measures and *public sector* capacity, the *Operator* shall take all *reasonable steps* to maintain a shared state of readiness for *tailings facility credible flow failure scenarios* by securing resources and carrying out annual training and exercises. The *Operator* shall conduct emergency response simulations at a frequency established in the *EPRP* but at least every 3 years for *tailings facilities* with potential loss of life.

Requirement 13.4   In the case of a *catastrophic tailings facility failure*, provide immediate response to save lives, supply humanitarian aid and minimise environmental harm.

PRINCIPLE 14   **PREPARE FOR LONG-TERM RECOVERY IN THE EVENT OF *CATASTROPHIC FAILURE*.**

Requirement 14.1   Based on *tailings facility credible flow failure scenarios* and the assessment of potential consequences, take *reasonable steps* to *meaningfully engage* with *public sector agencies* and other organisations that would participate in medium- and long-term social and environmental post-failure response strategies.

Requirement 14.2   In the event of a *catastrophic tailings facility failure*, assess social, environmental and local economic impacts as soon as possible after people are safe and short-term survival needs have been met.

Requirement 14.3   In the event of a *catastrophic tailings facility failure*, work with *public sector agencies* and other *stakeholders* to develop and implement reconstruction, *restoration* and recovery plans that address the medium- and long-term social, environmental and local economic impacts of the failure. The plans shall be disclosed if permitted by public authorities.

Requirement 14.4   In the event of a *catastrophic tailings facility failure*, enable the participation of affected people in reconstruction, *restoration* and recovery works and ongoing monitoring activities.

Requirement 14.5   Facilitate the monitoring and public reporting of post-failure outcomes that are aligned with the thresholds and indicators outlined in the reconstruction, *restoration* and recovery plans and adapt activities in response to findings and feedback.

PUBLIC DISCLOSURE AND ACCESS TO INFORMATION
TOPIC VI

PRINCIPLE 15   PUBLICLY DISCLOSE AND PROVIDE ACCESS TO INFORMATION ABOUT THE *TAILINGS FACILITY* TO SUPPORT PUBLIC ACCOUNTABILITY.

Requirement 15.1   Publish and regularly update information on the *Operator's* commitment to safe *tailings facility* management, implementation of its *tailings governance framework*, its organisation-wide policies, standards or approaches to the design, construction, monitoring and closure of *tailings facilities*.

A. For new *tailings facilities* for which the regulatory authorisation process has commenced, or that are otherwise approved by the *Operator*, the *Operator* shall publish and update, in accordance with Principle 21 of the UNGP, the following information:

1. A plain language summary of the rationale for the basis of the design and site selected as per the multi-criteria *alternatives analysis*, *impact assessments*, and mitigation plans (Information may be obtained from the output of multiple Requirements including, but not limited to, Requirements 3.2, 3.3, 5.1, 5.3, 6.4, 6.6, 7.1 and 10.1); and
2. The Consequence Classification. (Requirement 4.1).

B. For each existing *tailings facility* and in accordance with Principle 21 of the UNGP, the *Operator* shall publish and update at least on an annual basis, the following information:

1. A description of the *tailings facility* (information may be obtained from the output of Requirements 5.5 and 6.4);
2. The Consequence Classification (Requirement 4.1);
3. A summary of risk assessment findings relevant to the *tailings facility* (Information may be obtained from the output of Requirement 10.1);
4. A summary of *impact assessments* and of human exposure and vulnerability to *tailings facility credible flow failure scenarios* (Information may be obtained from the output of Requirements 2.4 and 3.3);
5. A description of the design for all phases of the *tailings facility lifecycle* including the current and final height (Information may be obtained from the output of Requirement 5.5);
6. A summary of *material* findings of annual performance reviews and *DSR*, including implementation of mitigation measures to reduce risk to *ALARP* (Information may be obtained from output of Requirements 10.4 and 10.5);
7. A summary of *material* findings of the environmental and social monitoring programme including implementation of mitigation measures (Requirement 7.5);
8. A summary version of the *tailings facility EPRP* for facilities that have a *credible failure mode(s)* that could lead to a flow failure event that: (i) is informed by *credible flow failure scenarios* from the *tailings facility breach analysis*; (ii) includes emergency response measures that apply

to *project affected people* as identified through the *tailings facility breach analysis* and involve cooperation with *public sector agencies*; and (iii) excludes details of emergency preparedness measures that apply to the *Operator's* assets, or confidential information (Requirements 13.1 and 13.2);

9. Dates of most recent and next independent reviews (Requirement 10.5); and

10. Annual confirmation that the *Operator* has adequate financial capacity (including insurance to the extent commercially reasonable) to cover estimated costs of planned closure, early closure, *reclamation*, and post-closure of the *tailings facility* and its appurtenant structures (Requirement 10.7).

Such disclosures shall be made directly, unless subject to limitations imposed by regulatory authorities.

C. Provide local authorities and emergency services with sufficient information derived from the *breach analysis* to enable effective disaster management planning (Information may be obtained from the output of Requirement 2.3);

Requirement 15.2   Respond in a systematic and timely manner to requests from interested and affected *stakeholders* for additional information *material* to the public safety and integrity of a *tailings facility*. When the request for information is denied, provide an explanation to the requesting *stakeholder*.

Requirement 15.3   Commit to cooperate in credible global transparency initiatives to create standardised, independent, industry-wide and publicly accessible databases, inventories or other information repositories about the safety and integrity of *tailings facilities*.

GLOSSARY

ANNEX 1

Terms shown throughout the Standard appear in italics and are explained below.

Accountable Executive	One or more executive(s) who is/are directly answerable to the CEO on matters related to this Standard, communicates with the Board of Directors, and who is accountable for the safety of tailings facilities and for minimising the social and environmental consequences of a potential tailings facility failure. The Accountable Executive(s) may delegate responsibilities but not accountability.
Adaptive Management	A structured, iterative process of robust decision-making with the aim of reducing uncertainty over time via system monitoring. It includes the implementation of mitigation and management measures that are responsive to changing conditions, including those related to climate change, and the results of monitoring throughout the tailings facility lifecycle. The approach supports alignment on decisions about the tailings facility with the changing social, environmental and economic context and enhances opportunities to develop resilience to climate change in the short and long term.
As Low As Reasonably Practicable	ALARP requires that all reasonable measures be taken with respect to 'tolerable' or acceptable risks to reduce them even further until the cost and other impacts of additional risk reduction are grossly disproportionate to the benefit.
Alternatives Analysis	An analysis that should objectively and rigorously consider all available options and sites for mine waste disposal. It should assess all aspects of each mine waste disposal alternative throughout the project life cycle (i.e. from construction through operation, closure and ultimately long-term monitoring and maintenance). The alternatives analysis should also include all aspects of the project that may contribute to the impacts associated with each potential alternative. The assessment should address environmental, technical and socio-economic aspects for each alternative throughout the project life cycle.
Best Practices	A procedure that has been shown by research and experience to produce optimal results and that is established or proposed as a standard suitable for widespread adoption.
Board of Directors	The ultimate governing body of the Operator typically elected by the shareholders of the Operator. The Board of Directors is the entity with the final decision-making authority for the Operator and holds the authority to, among other things, set the Operator's policies, objectives, and overall direction and oversee the firm's executives. As the term is used here, it encompasses any individual or entity with control over the Operator, including, for example, the owner or owners. Where the State serves as the Operator, the Board of Directors shall be understood to mean the government official with ultimate responsibility for the final decisions of the Operator.

Breach Analysis	A study that assumes a failure of the tailings facility and estimates its impact. Breach Analyses must be based on credible failure modes. The results should determine the physical area impacted by a potential failure, flow arrival times, depth and velocities, duration of flooding, and depth of material deposition. The Breach Analysis is based on scenarios which are not connected to probability of occurrence. It is primarily used to inform emergency preparedness and response planning and the consequence of failure classification. The classification is then used to inform the external loading component of the design criteria.
Catastrophic Failure	A tailings facility failure that results in material disruption to social, environmental and local economic systems. Such failures are a function of the interaction between hazard exposure, vulnerability, and the capacity of people and systems to respond. Catastrophic events typically involve numerous adverse impacts, at different scales and over different timeframes, including loss of life, damage to physical infrastructure or natural assets, and disruption to lives, livelihoods, and social order. Operators may be affected by damage to assets, disruption to operations, financial loss, or negative impact to reputation. Catastrophic failures exceed the capacity of affected people to cope using their own resources, triggering the need for outside assistance in emergency response, restoration and recovery efforts.
Change Management System	Changes in projects are inevitable during design construction and operation and must be managed to reduce negative impacts to quality and integrity of the tailings facility. The impact and consequences of changes vary according to the type and nature of changes, but most importantly according to how they are managed. Managing changes effectively is crucial to the success of a project. A change management system has the objective of disciplining and coordinating the process, and should include an evaluation of the change, a review and formal approval of the change followed by detailed documentation including drawings and, where required, changes to equipment, process, actions, flow, information, cost, schedule or personnel.
Construction versus Design Intent Verification	Intended to ensure the design intent is implemented and still being met if the site conditions vary from the design assumptions. The CDIV identifies any discrepancies between the field conditions and the design assumptions, such that the design can be adjusted to account for the actual field conditions.
Construction Records Report	Describes all aspects of the 'as-built' product, including all geometrical information, materials, laboratory and field test results, construction activities, schedule, equipment and procedures, Quality Control and Quality Assurance data, CDIV results, changes to design or any aspect of construction, non-conformances and their resolution, construction photographs, construction shift reports, and any other relevant information. Instruments and their installation details, calibration records and readings must be included in the CRR. Roles, responsibilities and personnel, including independent review should be documented. Detailed construction record drawings are fundamental.
Corporate Governance	Refers to the organisational structures and processes that a company puts in place to ensure effective management, oversight and accountability.

Credible Failure Modes / Scenarios	Refers to technically feasible failure mechanisms given the materials present in the structure and its foundation, the properties of these materials, the configuration of the structure, drainage conditions and surface water control at the facility, throughout its lifecycle. Credible failure modes can and do typically vary during the lifecycle of the facility as the conditions vary. A facility that is appropriately designed and operated considers all of these credible failure modes and includes sufficient resilience against each. Different failure modes will result in different failure scenarios. Credible catastrophic failure modes do not exist for all tailings facilities. The term 'credible failure mode' is not associated with a probability of this event occurring and having credible failure modes is not a reflection of facility safety.
Critical Controls	A control that is critical to preventing a potential undesirable event or mitigating the consequences of such an event. The absence or failure of a critical control would disproportionately increase the risk despite the existence of the other controls.
Cross-functional	A system or a practice whereby people from different areas of an organisation share information and work together effectively as a team.
Dam Safety Review	A periodic and systematic process carried out by an independent qualified review engineer to assess and evaluate the safety of a dam or system of dams (or in this case a tailings facility) against failure modes, in order to make a statement on the safety of the facility. A safe tailings facility is one that performs its intended function under both normal and unusual conditions; does not impose an unacceptable risk to people, property or environment; and meets applicable safety criteria.
Design Basis Report	Provides the basis for the design, operation, construction, monitoring and risk management of a tailings facility.
Designer of Record	A qualified professional engineer designated by the Engineer of Record to design the tailings facility in the case where the Engineer of Record is an internal professional.
Deviance Accountability Report	Provides an assessment of the cumulative impact of changes to the tailings facility on the risk level of the achieved product and defines the potential requirement for updates to the design, DBR, OMS or the monitoring programme.
Emergency Preparedness and Response Plan	A site-specific plan developed to identify hazards, assess capacity and prepare for an emergency based on tailings facility credible flow failure scenarios, and to respond if it occurs. This may be part of operation-wide emergency response planning and includes the identification of response capacity and any necessary coordination with off-site emergency responders, local communities and public sector agencies. The development of the EPRP includes a community-focused planning process to support the co-development and implementation of emergency response measures by those vulnerable to a tailings facility failure.

Engineer of Record	The qualified engineering firm responsible for confirming that the tailings facility is designed, constructed, and decommissioned with appropriate concern for integrity of the facility, and that it aligns with and meets applicable regulations, statutes, guidelines, codes, and standards. The Engineer of Record may delegate responsibility but not accountability. In some highly-regulated jurisdictions, notably Japan, the role of EOR is undertaken by the responsible regulatory authorities.
Environmental and Social Management System	A methodological approach which draws on the elements of the established process of 'Plan, Do, Check, Act', and is used to manage environmental and social risks and impacts in a structured way in the short and longer term.
	An effective ESMS, appropriate to the nature and scale of the operation, promotes sound and sustainable environmental and social performance, and can also lead to improved financial outcomes. The ESMS helps companies integrate the procedures and objectives for the management of social, environmental (and, local economic) impacts into core business operations, through a set of clearly defined, repeatable processes. An ESMS is a dynamic and continuous process initiated and supported by management, and involves engagement between the Operator, its employees and contractors, project-affected people and, where appropriate, other stakeholders. The interaction of the ESMS with the TMS facilitates alignment of decisions about the tailings facility with the changing social, environmental and local economic context and reflects the fact that a tailings facility is situated within a complex and dynamic local and global environment.
Free, Prior and Informed Consent	A mechanism that safeguards the individual and collective rights of indigenous and tribal peoples, including their land and resource rights and their right to self-determination. The minimum conditions that are required to secure consent include that it is 'free' from all forms of coercion, undue influence or pressure, provided 'prior' to a decision or action being taken that affects individual and collective human rights, and offered on the basis that affected peoples are 'informed' of their rights and the impacts of decisions or actions on those rights. FPIC is considered to be an ongoing process of negotiation, subject to an initial consent. To obtain FPIC, 'consent' must be secured through an agreed process of good faith consultation and cooperation with indigenous and tribal peoples through their own representative institutions. The process should be grounded in a recognition that the indigenous or tribal peoples are customary landowners. FPIC is not only a question of process, but also of outcome, and is obtained when terms are fully respectful of land, resource and other implicated rights.
Grievance	A perceived injustice, which may be based on law, contract, explicit or implicit promises, customary practice, or general notions of fairness of aggrieved communities.
Hazard	Any substance, human activity, condition or other agent that may cause harm, loss of life, injury, health impacts, loss of integrity of natural or built structures, property damage, loss of livelihoods or services, social and economic disruption, or environmental damage.

Impact Assessment	A decision-making and management support instrument for identifying, predicting, measuring and evaluating the impact of development proposals, both prior to major decisions being made, and throughout the lifecycle of a project. While impact assessments typically focus on a single project, assessments can be scoped at the landscape level, and consider strategic implications of a change. Depending on the context, the circumstances, and the issues at hand, impact assessments may be discipline-specific, or conducted as part of an integrated set of studies. Assessments can be conducted in advance of impacts, or retrospectively.
	In this context, impacts are consequences to people, built infrastructure or the natural environment caused by a tailings facility or its failure, including impacts to the human rights of workers, communities, or other rights holders and including sensitive ecological receptors and ecosystem services. Impacts can be positive or adverse, tangible or intangible, direct or indirect, acute, chronic or cumulative, and measurable quantitatively or qualitatively.
Independent Tailings Review Board	A board that provides independent technical review of the design, construction, operation, closure and management of tailings facilities. The independent reviewers are third-parties who are not, and have not been directly involved with the design or operation of the particular tailings facility. The expertise of the ITRB members shall reflect the range of issues relevant to the facility and its context and the complexity of these issues. In some highly regulated jurisdictions, notably Japan, the role of ITRB is undertaken by the responsible regulatory authorities.
Involuntary Resettlement	Resettlement can be either voluntary or involuntary, and may involve either physical or economic displacement. Involuntary resettlement occurs when project-affected people do not have the right to refuse resettlement. This includes cases where a company has the legal right to expropriate land. Voluntary resettlement occurs when resettled households have a genuine choice to move. When the voluntary nature of resettlement cannot be confirmed, resettlement should be treated as involuntary.
Knowledge Base	The sum of knowledge required to support the safe management of a tailings facility throughout its lifecycle. The knowledge base has an iterative nature and needs to be updated as the need arises and the context changes. Fundamental elements would include a detailed site characterisation and baseline knowledge of the social and environmental context. As design, construction and performance monitoring proceeds additional data are collected and required and the knowledge base evolves.
Material (adj)	Important enough to merit attention, or having an effective influence or bearing on the determination in question. For the Standard, the criteria for what is material will be defined by Operator, subject to the provisions of local regulations, and evaluated as part of any audit or external independent assessment that may be conducted on implementation.

Meaningful Engagement	A process of mutual dialogue and decision-making whereby Operators have an obligation to consult and listen to stakeholder perspectives, and integrate those perspectives into their business decisions. Meaningful engagement involves measures to overcome structural and practical barriers to the participation of diverse and vulnerable groups of people. Strategies for addressing barriers must be appropriate to the context and the stakeholders involved, and may include, for example, logistics and other support to enable participation. Preconditions to meaningful engagement include: access to material information that can be reasonably understood; a structure that enables transparent communication; and accountability for engagement processes and outcomes.
Mitigation Hierarchy	Identifies a series of essential, sequential steps that Operators must follow through the project lifecycle in order to limit negative impacts and to enhance opportunities for positive outcomes. It describes a process to anticipate and avoid adverse impacts on workers, communities and the environment from a proposed action. Where avoidance is not possible, actions must be taken to minimise, and where residual impacts remain, to compensate fairly or offset for the risks and impacts.
Observational Method	A continuous, managed, integrated, process of design, construction control, monitoring and review that enables previously defined modifications to be incorporated during or after construction as appropriate. All of these aspects must be demonstrably robust. The key element of the Observational Method is the proactive assessment at the design stage of every possible unfavourable situation that might be disclosed by the monitoring programme and the development of an action plan or mitigative measure to reduce risk in case the unfavourable situation is observed. This element forms the basis of a performance-based risk management approach. The objective is to achieve greater overall safety. See Peck, R.B. (1969) "Advantages and Limitations of the Observational Method in Applied Soil Mechanics" Geotechnique 19, No2., pp.171-187.
Operations, Maintenance and Surveillance Manual	Describes the performance indicators and criteria for risk controls and critical controls, and the ranges of performance linked to specific pre-defined management actions. An OMS manual also describes the procedures for collecting, analysing and reporting surveillance results in a manner consistent with the risk controls and critical controls and that supports effective, timely decision-making. The link between OMS activities and critical controls management underscores the fact that it is essential that OMS Manuals be developed to reflect site-specific conditions and circumstances. An OMS Manual cannot be purchased 'off-the-shelf'. To be effective, it must be tailored to the site.
Operator	An entity that singly, or jointly with other entities, exercises ultimate control of a tailings facility. This may include a corporation, partnership, owner, affiliate, subsidiary, joint venture, or other entity, including any State agency, that controls a tailings facility.

Preliminary Design	For the purpose of Requirement 4.2 of the Standard , preliminary design is a design performed to a level of detail sufficient to determine the differences between viable designs that adopt different external loading design criteria in terms of required footprints, volumes and drainage requirements.
Project-affected People	People who may experience impacts from a tailings facility. People affected by a tailings facility may include, for example, people who live nearby; people who hear, smell or see the facility; or people who might own, reside on, or use the land on which the facility is to be located or may potentially inundate.
Public Sector Agencies	All governmental agencies at the State, regional, and/or local level with some responsibility or authority for regulating mining activities that occur within or impact their jurisdictions.
Reasonable Steps	Steps taken to achieve a specific objective such that any negative impact on people, social systems, environment, local economy or costs is not out of balance with the intended benefits.
Reclamation	The process of restoring the mine site to a natural or economically useable state as provided in a reclamation plan. Reclamation results in productive and sustainable landscapes to meet a range of conditions that might allow for biodiversity conservation, recreational or agriculture uses, or various forms of economic development.
Responsible Tailings Facility Engineer	An engineer appointed by the Operator to be responsible for the tailings facility. The RTFE must be available at all times during construction, operations and closure. The RTFE has clearly defined, delegated responsibility for management of the tailings facility and has appropriate qualifications and experience compatible with the level of complexity of the tailings facility. The RTFE is responsible for the scope of work and budget requirements for the tailings facility, including risk management. The RTFE may delegate specific tasks and responsibilities for aspects of tailings management to qualified personnel but not accountability.
Restoration	The process of assisting recovery of the social, environmental and local economic systems that have been degraded, damaged or destroyed.
Robust Design	The robustness of a tailings facility design depends on each particular situation and it may be associated with various aspects including, for example, the factor of safety against each of the potential failure modes, the presence or absence of materials with brittle behaviour, the degree of brittleness of these materials, the degree of variability of the materials and the potential for thresholds of deformation that materially affect the facility performance. The degree of robustness is related to the facility maintaining its overall integrity despite less than ideal performance of one or more of its components.
Safe closure	A closed tailings facility that does not pose ongoing material risks to people or the environment which has been confirmed by an ITRB or senior independent technical reviewer and signed off by the Accountable Executive.

Senior Independent Technical Reviewer	An independent professional with in-depth knowledge and at least 15 years' experience in the specific area of the review requirements, e.g. tailings design, operations and closure, environmental and social aspects or any other specific topic of concern. The independent reviewer is a third-party who is not, and has not been directly involved with the design or operation of the particular tailings facility.
Senior Technical Reviewer	A professional who is either an in-house employee or an external party with in-depth knowledge and at least 15 years' experience in the specific area of the review requirements, e.g. tailings design, operations and closure, environmental and social aspects or any other specific topic of concern.
Stakeholder	Persons or groups who are directly or indirectly affected by a project, as well as those who may have interests in a project and/or the ability to influence its outcome, positively or negatively. Stakeholders may include workers, trade unions, project-affected people or communities and their formal and informal representatives, national or local government authorities, politicians, religious leaders, civil society organisations and groups with special interests, the academic community, or other businesses. Different stakeholders will often have divergent views, both within and across stakeholder groupings.
Tailings	A by-product of mining, consisting of the processed rock or soil left over from the separation of the commodities of value from the rock or soil within which they occur.
Tailings Facility	A facility that is designed and managed to contain the tailings produced by the mine. Although tailings can be placed in mined-out underground mines, for the purposes of the Standard, tailings facilities refer to facilities that contain tailings in open pit mines or on the surface ('external tailings facilities').

For the purposes of the Standard, tailings facilities are higher than 2.5 m measured from the elevation of the crest to the elevation of the toe of the structure, or have a combined water and solids volume more than 30,000 m3, unless the Consequence Classification is 'High', 'Very High' or 'Extreme', in which case the structure is considered a tailings facility regardless of its size.

For the purposes of this Standard, existing tailings facilities are facilities that are accepting new mine tailings on the date that the Standard takes effect or not currently accepting new mine tailings but are not in a state of safe closure.

All other facilities will be treated as New for the purposes of this Standard.

Tailings Facility Lifecycle	The phases in the life of a facility, which may occur in linear or cyclical succession, consisting of: 1. Project conception, planning and design; 2. Initial construction; 3. Operation and ongoing construction (may include progressive reclamation); 4. Interim closure (including care and maintenance); 5. Closure (regrading, demolition and reclamation); 6. Post-closure (including relinquishment, reprocessing, relocation, removal)
Tailings Governance Framework	A framework that focusses on the key elements of management and governance necessary to maintain the integrity of TSFs and minimise the risk of catastrophic failures. The six key elements of this TSF governance framework are: 1. Accountability, Responsibility and Competency; 2. Planning and Resourcing; 3. Risk Management; 4. Change Management; 5. Emergency Preparedness and Response; 6. Review and Assurance.
Tailings Management System	The site-specific TMS comprises the key components for management and design of the tailings facility and is often referred to as the 'framework' that manages these components. The TMS sits at the core of the Standard and is focused on the safe operation and management of the tailings facility throughout its lifecycle (see above). The TMS follows the well-established Plan-Do-Check-Act cycle. Each Operator develops a TMS that best suits their organisation and tailings facilities. A TMS includes elements such as: establishing policies, planning, designing and establishing performance objectives, managing change, identifying and securing adequate resources (experienced and/or qualified personnel, equipment, scheduling, data, documentation and financial resources), conducting performance evaluations and risk assessments, establishing and implementing controls for risk management, auditing and reviewing for continual improvement, implementing a management system with clear accountabilities and responsibilities, preparing and implementing the OMS and EPRP. The TMS, and its various elements, must interact with other systems, such as the environmental and social management system (ESMS), the operation-wide management system, and the regulatory system. This systems interaction is fundamental to the effective implementation of the Standard.
Trigger Action Response Plan	A TARP is a tool to manage risk controls, including critical controls. TARPs provide pre-defined trigger levels for performance criteria that are based on the risk controls and critical controls of the tailings facility. The trigger levels are developed based on the performance objectives and risk management plan for the tailings facility. TARPs describe actions to be taken if trigger levels are exceeded (performance is outside the normal range), to prevent a loss of control. A range of actions is pre-defined, based on the magnitude of the exceedance of the trigger level.

CONSEQUENCE CLASSIFICATION TABLES

ANNEX 2

Table 1: Consequence Classification Matrix

Dam Failure Consequence Classification	Potential Population at Risk	Potential Loss of Life	
Low	None	None expected	
Significant	1–10	Unspecified	
High	10–100	Possible (1–10)	
Very High	100–1,000	Likely (10 – 100)	
Extreme	> 1,000	Many (> 100)	

| Incremental Losses | | |
Environment	Health, Social and Cultural	Infrastructure and Economics
Minimal short-term loss or deterioration of habitat or rare and endangered species.	Minimal effects and disruption of business and livelihoods. No measurable effect on human health. No disruption of heritage, recreation, community or cultural assets.	Low economic losses: area contains limited infrastructure or services. <US$1M.
No significant loss or deterioration of habitat. Potential contamination of livestock/fauna water supply with no health effects. Process water low potential toxicity. Tailings not potentially acid generating and have low neutral leaching potential. Restoration possible within 1 to 5 years.	Significant disruption of business, service or social dislocation. Low likelihood of loss of regional heritage, recreation, community, or cultural assets. Low likelihood of health effects.	Losses to recreational facilities, seasonal workplaces, and infrequently used transportation routes. <US$10M.
Significant loss or deterioration of critical habitat or rare and endangered species. Potential contamination of livestock/fauna water supply with no health effects. Process water moderately toxic. Low potential for acid rock drainage or metal leaching effects of released tailings. Potential area of impact 10 km^2 – 20 km^2. Restoration possible but difficult and could take > 5 years.	500-1,000 people affected by disruption of business, services or social dislocation. Disruption of regional heritage, recreation, community or cultural assets. Potential for short term human health effects.	High economic losses affecting infrastructure, public transportation, and commercial facilities, or employment. Moderate relocation/compensation to communities. <US$100M.
Major loss or deterioration of critical habitat or rare and endangered species. Process water highly toxic. High potential for acid rock drainage or metal leaching effects from released tailings. Potential area of impact > 20 km^2. Restoration or compensation possible but very difficult and requires a long time (5 years to 20 years).	1,000 people affected by disruption of business, services or social dislocation for more than one year. Significant loss of national heritage, community or cultural assets. Potential for significant long-term human health effects.	Very high economic losses affecting important infrastructure or services (e.g., highway, industrial facility, storage facilities, for dangerous substances), or employment. High relocation/compensation to communities. < US$1B.
Catastrophic loss of critical habitat or rare and endangered species. Process water highly toxic. Very high potential for acid rock drainage or metal leaching effects from released tailings. Potential area of impact > 20 km^2. Restoration or compensation in kind impossible or requires a very long time (> 20 years).	5,000 people affected by disruption of business, services or social dislocation for years. Significant National heritage or community facilities or cultural assets destroyed. Potential for severe and/or long- term human health effects.	Extreme economic losses affecting critical infrastructure or services, (e.g., hospital, major industrial complex, major storage facilities for dangerous substances) or employment. Very high relocation/compensation to communities and very high social readjustment costs. >US$1B.

The intention of this guidance is to provide a consistent manner to establish minimum external loading design criteria for the safe design of *tailings facilities*. Alternative guidance exists, for example, by reputable national dam associations, which, in turn, form the basis of jurisdictional regulatory requirements. These alternative guidances can be considered by the *EOR*, *RTFE* and *ITRB* or independent technical reviewer and adopted, if appropriate and approved by the *Accountable Executive*.

There is a distinction between Operations and Post-Closure (also referred to as Passive Care Closure) where Operations involves all phases of construction and operation, periods of temporary cessation of operations, and the Closure phase (transition phase into post-closure also referred to as active care closure). Post-Closure refers to permanently closed facilities that have been configured for their perpetual form/state and thereby will be subjected to the maximum time of exposure irrespective of the Consequence Classification for the facility.

Table 2: Flood Design Criteria

Consequence Classification	Flood Criteria[1] – Annual Exceedance Probability	
	Operations and Closure (Active care)	Passive-Closure (Passive Care)
Low	1/200	1/10,000
Significant	1/1,000	1/10,000
High	1/2,475	1/10,000
Very High	1/5,000	1/10,000
Extreme	1/10,000	1/10,000

The term "Maximum Probable Precipitation" (PMP) or "Probable Maximum Flood" (PMF) are terms sometimes used to denote extreme hydrological events. The concepts of PMP and PMF are acceptable for assigning flood loading if they meet, or exceed, the requirements above for Extreme Consequence Classification facilities and/or facilities at the Post-Closure (or Passive Care Closure) phase.

Table 3: Seismic Design Criteria

Consequence Classification	Seismic Criteria[2,3] – Annual Exceedance Probability	
	Operations and Closure (Active care)	Passive-Closure (Passive Care)
Low	1/200[2]	1/10,000[2]
Significant	1/1,000[2]	1/10,000[2]
High	1/2,475[2]	1/10,000[2]
Very High	1/5,000[2]	1/10,000[2]
Extreme	1/10,000[2]	1/10,000[2]

1. For existing *tailings facilities* the *EOR*, with review by the *ITRB* or a *senior independent technical reviewer*, may determine that the upgrade to this design criteria is not feasible or cannot be retroactively applied. In this case, the *Accountable Executive* shall approve and document the implementation of measures to reduce both the probability and the consequences of a *tailings facility* failure in order to reduce the risk to a level *as low as reasonably practicable (ALARP)*. The basis and timing for addressing the upgrade of existing *tailings facilities* shall be risk-informed and carried out as soon as reasonably practicable (see Requirement 4.7).

2. The selection of the design ground motion should consider the seismic setting and the reliability and applicability of the probabilistic and deterministic methods for seismic *hazard* assessment. The Maximum Credible Earthquake (MCE) is part of a deterministic approach that can govern in some areas. The method that produces the most appropriate ground motion for the facility safety should be used for the design.

3. For existing *tailings facilities* the *EOR*, with review by the *ITRB* or a *senior independent technical reviewer*, may determine that the upgrade to this design criteria is not feasible or cannot be retroactively applied. In this case, the *Accountable Executive* shall approve and document the implementation of measures to reduce both the probability and the consequences of a *tailings facility* failure in order to reduce the risk to a level *as low as reasonably practicable (ALARP)*. The basis and timing for addressing the upgrade of existing *tailings facilities* shall be risk-informed and carried out as soon as reasonably practicable (see Requirement 4.7).

SUMMARY TABLES

ANNEX 3

Table 4: Summary of Key Roles and Functions mentioned in the Standard

Key Role	Function
	Items listed below are either expressly requested in the Standard OR are listed against those roles which typically undertake these activities. It is understood that this may vary depending on the operation.
Responsible Tailings Facility Engineer (RTFE)	• Accountable for the integrity of the *tailings facility* (Requirement 8.5). • Responsible for liaising with *EOR*, operations, planning, regulatory affairs, social performance and environment teams (Requirement 8.5). • Responsible for implementation of the design. • Accountable for the establishment of a *change management system* (Requirement 6.5). • Responsible for the monitoring system and communication of the results to the *EOR*, including performance reviews (Requirements 7.2, 7.3). • Responsible, with the *EOR*, for the *Construction Records Report* (Requirement 6.3). • Responsible for the *OMS Manual* (Requirement 6.4).
Engineer of Record (EoR)	• Responsible for the *Design Basis Report* (Requirement 4.8). • Responsible for the design (Requirement 9.1). • Responsible for the design report. • Responsible for construction and performance reviews (Requirement 10.4). • Responsible for the *Deviance Accountability Report* (Requirement 6.5). • Responsible, with the *RTFE*, for the *Construction Records Report* (Requirement 6.3). • Support the *RTFE* on the *OMS Manual* (Requirement 6.4).
Accountable Executive	• Accountable for the safety of the *tailings facility* and for environmental and social performance (Requirements 7.1, 8.2, 8.3, 8.4). • Approval of the adopted design criteria and measures to reduce the risk of failure of existing facilities to *ALARP* (Requirements 4.3, 4.7, 5.7). • Accountable for *tailings* management training, emergency preparedness and response (Requirement 8.4). • Selection of the *RTFE* (Requirements 8.5, 8.6) and the *EOR* (Requirements 9.1 to 9.5, 8.6). • Appointment of the *ITRB* or a *senior independent technical reviewer* (Requirement 8.7). • Establishment of a process for addressing concerns (Requirement 12.1).
Independent Tailings Review Board (ITRB) or senior technical reviewer	• Review of the design, construction, risk assessments, *governance* systems and other risk management matters that can affect the *tailings facility*, ensuring that the required expertise and skill sets are involved. • Review of the adopted external loading design criteria and measures to reduce the risk of failure of existing facilities to *ALARP* (Requirements 4.2, 4.7, 5.7). • Review of the *alternatives analysis* (Requirement 3.2), design, construction, risk assessments (Requirements 10.1), governance systems and other risk management matters (Requirement 10.6) that can affect the *tailings facility*. • Review the *Design Basis Report* (Requirement 4.8). • Determine the frequency of *Dam Safety Review* (Requirement 10.5).

Table 5: Summary of Key Documents mentioned in the Standard

Key Documents	Description
Design Basis Report	Details the design assumptions and criteria, including operational constraints to provide a basis for all phases of the *tailings facility lifecycle*.
Design Report	Includes among other items: documentation of the relevant aspects of *knowledge base*, the consequence classification, multi-criteria *alternatives analysis*, water balance modelling, design analyses and evaluation of their results, design of all stages of the facility including monitoring requirements, construction requirements and specifications, operational constraints and construction drawings. The Design Report typically includes constuction drawings.
Construction Records Report	Includes among other items: survey data and drawings, field reports, QC and QA reports, *CDIV* reports, changes required during construction, drilling and field test data, instrumentation installation details and calibration reports, instrumentation monitoring data, description of field procedures and equipment, photographic records (Requirements 6.2, 6.3, 6.5).
Operation, Maintenance and Surveillance Manual	Provides the context and *critical controls* for the safe operation of the *tailings facility* to support effective risk management. Includes among other items: description of the facility, (Requirements 6.4, 6.5). It includes the *Trigger Action Response Plan (TARP)*.
Deviance Accountability Report	Provides an assessment of the cumulative impact of the individual changes assessed, approved and documented in the *change management system*, on the risk level of the as-constructed *tailings facility* and provides recommendations for managing the risk, if required.
Annual Performance Report	Provides the results of the annual performance review and typically includes results of visual inspection, instrumentation monitoring and assessment. Some *Operators* may conduct internal performance reports on a more frequent basis.
Dam Safety Review Report	Provides the results of a review of the safety of a *tailings facility* covering technical, operational and governance aspects, conducted by an independent technical specialist according to established *best practices*.
Emergency Preparedness and Response Plan (EPRP)	Provides a detailed, site-specific plan developed to identify *hazards* of the *tailings facility*, assess capacity internally and externally to respond, and prepare for an emergency and to respond if it occurs.
Impact Assessments and Mitigation Plans	Assessments of the social, environmental and local economic impacts from a *tailings facility* or its failure, and the associated impact mitigation and management plans.

Table 6: Summary of Levels of Review mentioned in the Standard

Key Documents	Description
Internal Reviews	Includes reviews of company processes, procedures, guidelines and *corporate governance* requirements and systems (including *TMS, ESMS*) (Requirement 10.3).
EoR Review	Engineering firms typically have internal review systems for all engineering work to manage the accuracy and quality of the technical product and provide mentoring and training to staff. This is also good practice for technical work done in-house by the *Operator* (Requirement 9.3).
Annual Performance Reviews	Conducted by the *EOR* or an independent reviewer. Regular performance reviews are typically mandated in many jurisdictions, often annually or twice a year. Some *Operators* may conduct internal performance reviews more frequently. These reviews typically involve visual inspection, review of construction and operation practices and review and assessment of the instrumentation monitoring data.
Dam Safety Review (DSR)	Independent review of the safety of a *tailings facility* covering technical, operational and governance aspects, conducted by an independent technical specialist according to established *best practices*. It should be conducted at intervals based on the Consequence Classification and the complexity of its condition or performance. It is regulatory requirement in many jurisdictions.
Independent Tailings Review Board (ITRB) or Senior Technical Reviewer	Provides ongoing senior independent review of the planning, siting, design, construction, operation, maintenance, monitoring, performance, risk management at appropriate intervals across all phases of the *tailings facility lifecycle* (Requirement 8.8).

Co-convened by the International Council on
Mining and Metals (ICMM), United Nations
Environment Programme (UNEP) and Principles for
Responsible Investment (PRI), the Global Tailings
Review has established a robust, fit-for-purpose
international standard for the safer management of
tailings storage facilities.

Co-convened by

Index